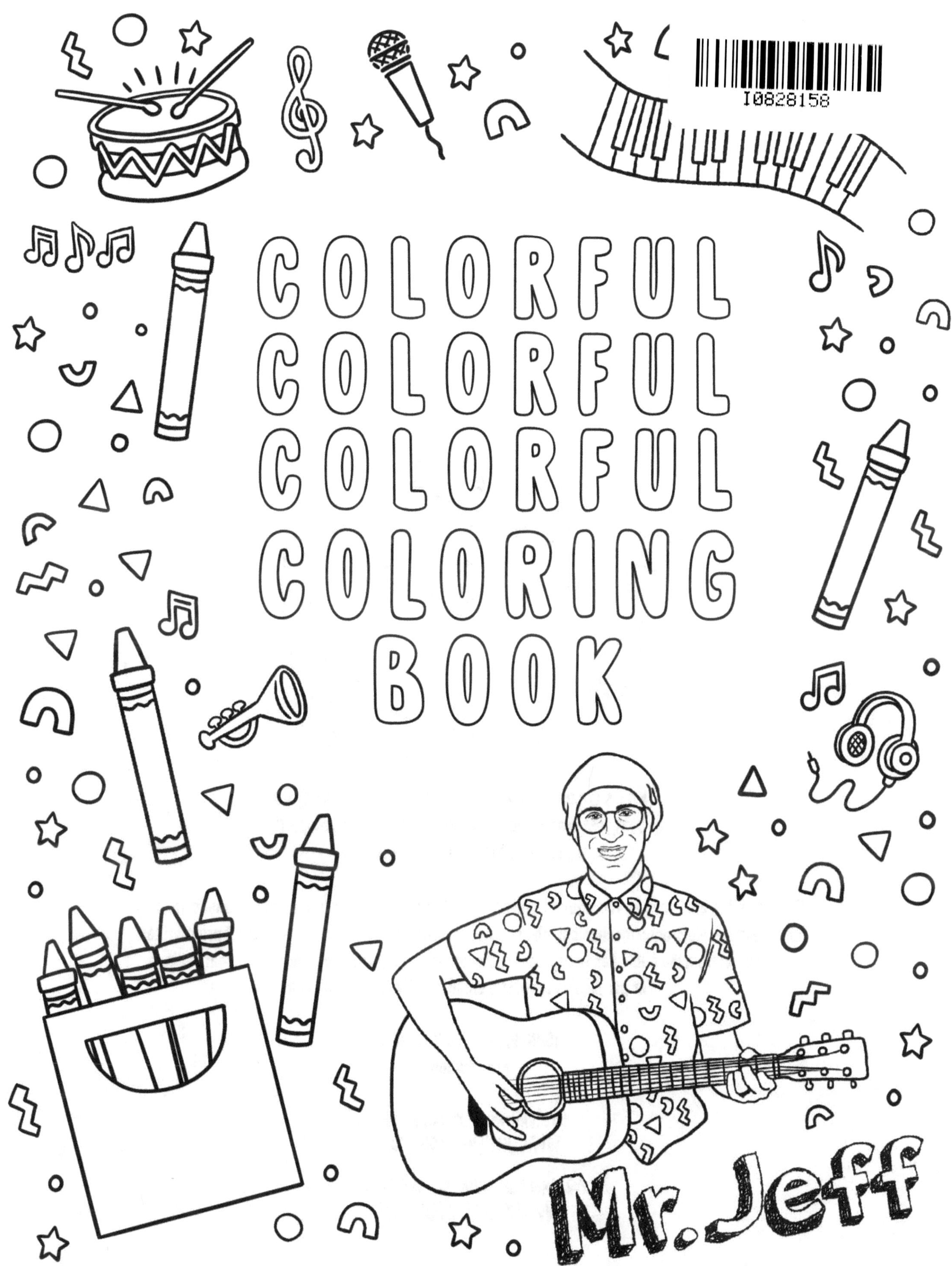
I0828158
COLORFUL
COLORFUL
COLORFUL
COLORING
BOOK
Mr. Jeff

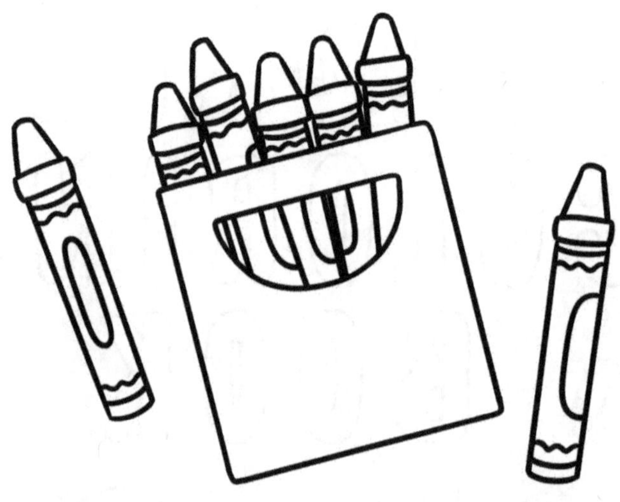

MR. JEFF'S COLORFUL COLORFUL COLORFUL COLORING BOOK

PUBLISHED BY JILLYJELLY PRESS

ISBN: 979-8-9988443-0-0
First Edition

ILLUSTRATIONS BY JILLIAN KLEMM:
WWW.JILLYJELLYART.COM

FOR MORE FUN, MUSIC, AND LEARNING:
WWW.MRJEFFISFUN.COM

THIS BOOK BELONGS TO:

....

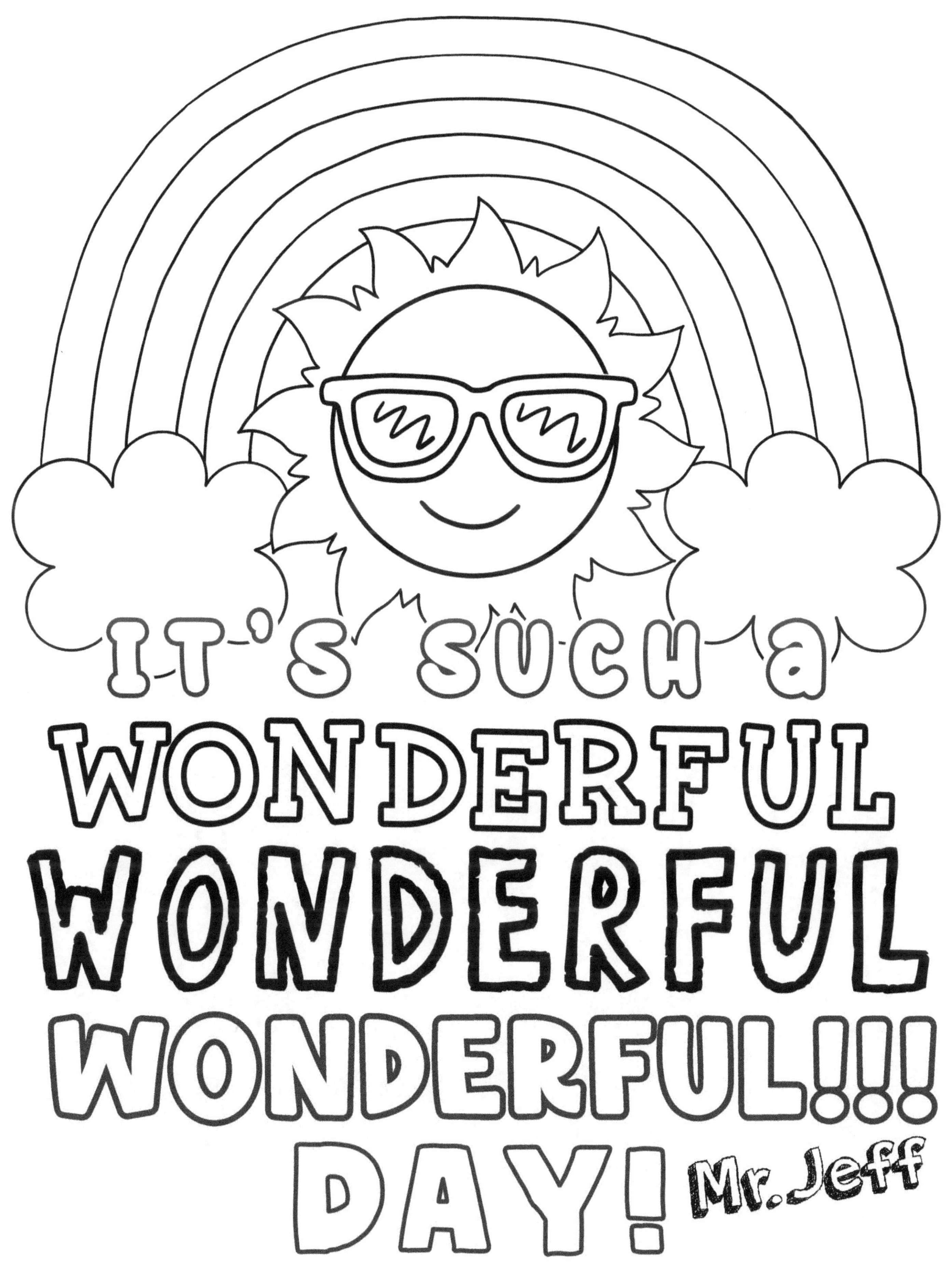
IT'S SUCH a
WONDERFUL
WONDERFUL
WONDERFUL!!!
DAY!
Mr. Jeff

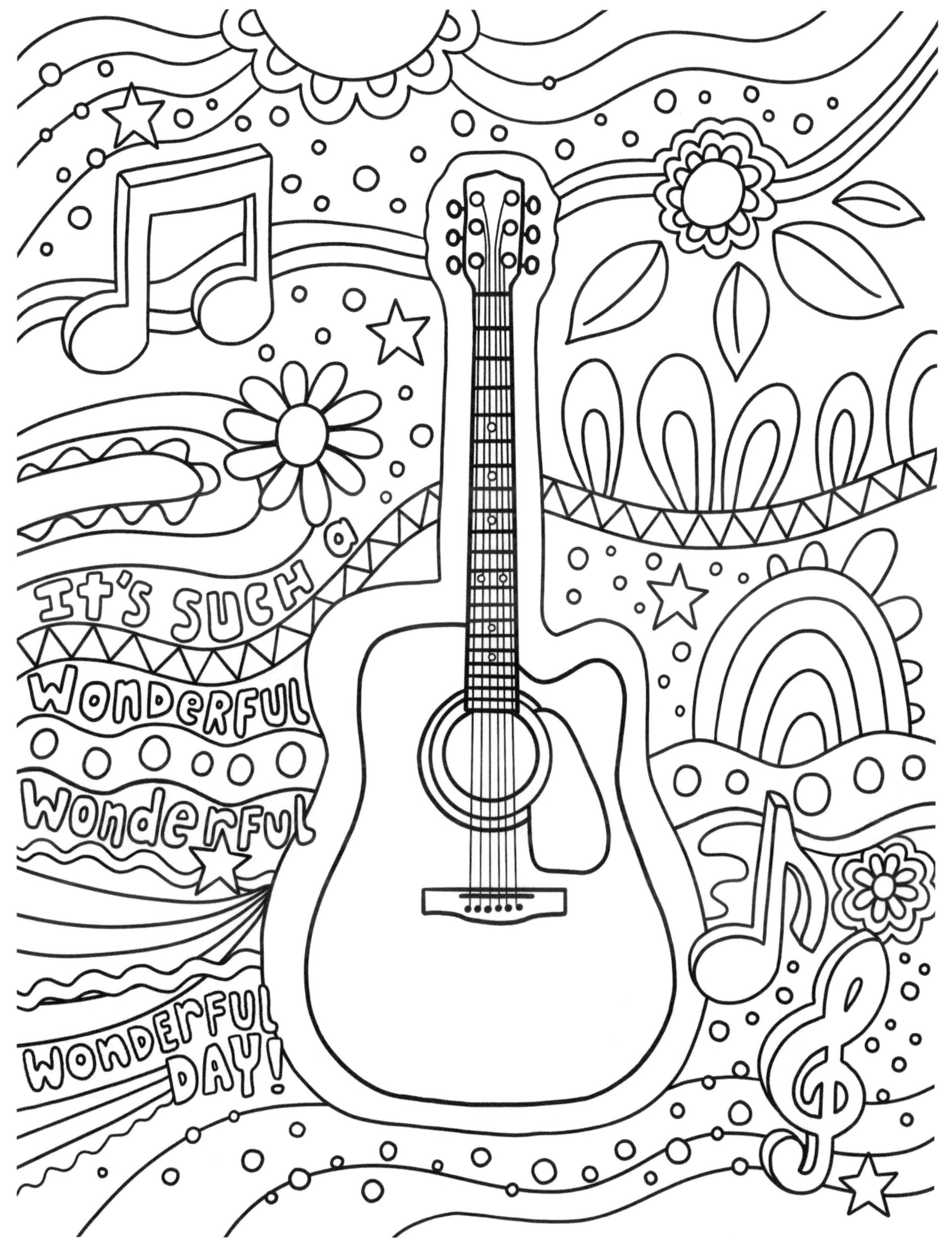
It's such a
wonderful
wonderful
wonderful
day!

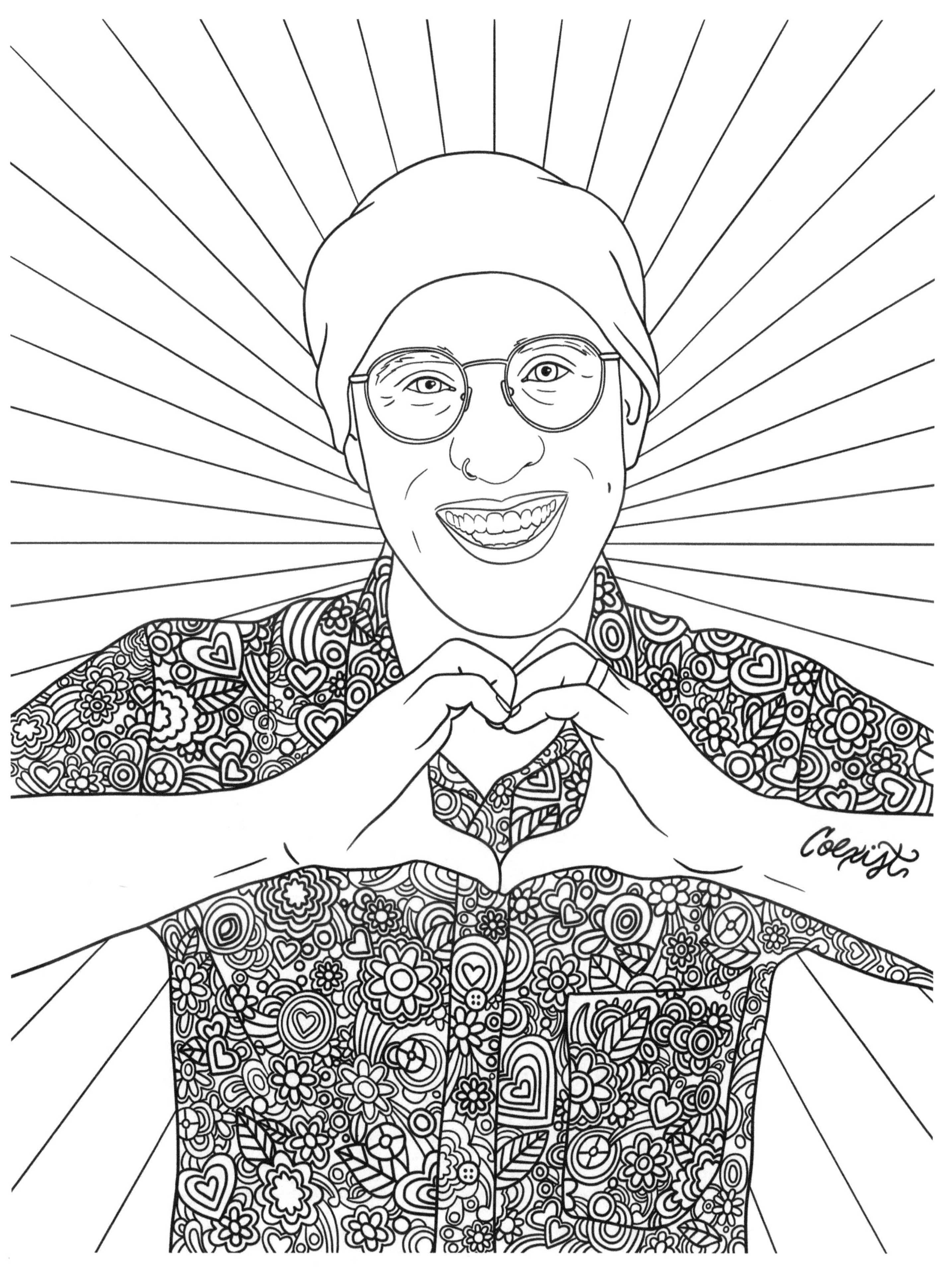

SMILE
XOXO
DRAW A PICTURE OF YOURSELF
WITH YOUR BEST SMILE

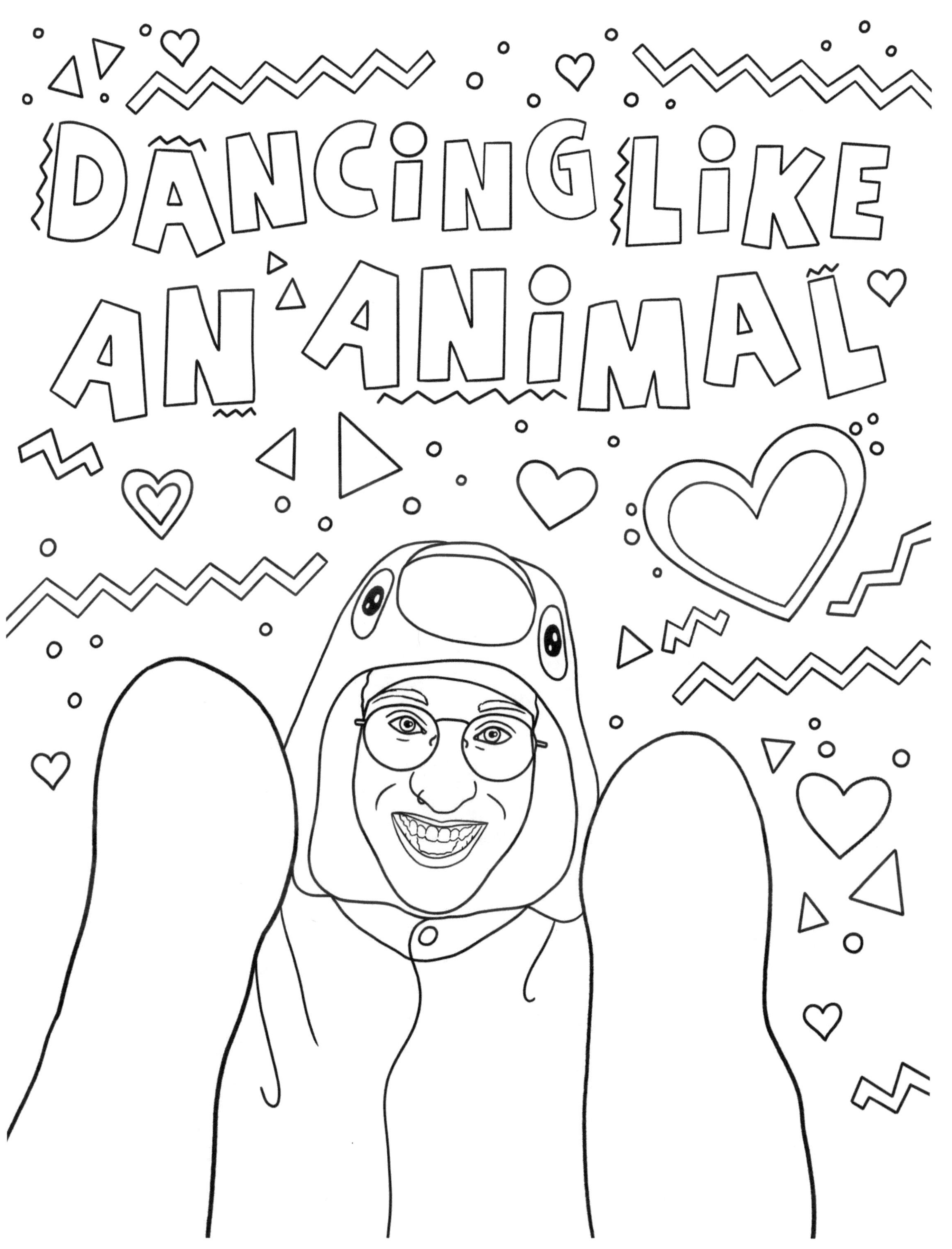
DANCING LIKE
AN ANIMAL

CAN YOU MATCH EACH ANIMAL WITH ITS DANCE MOVE?

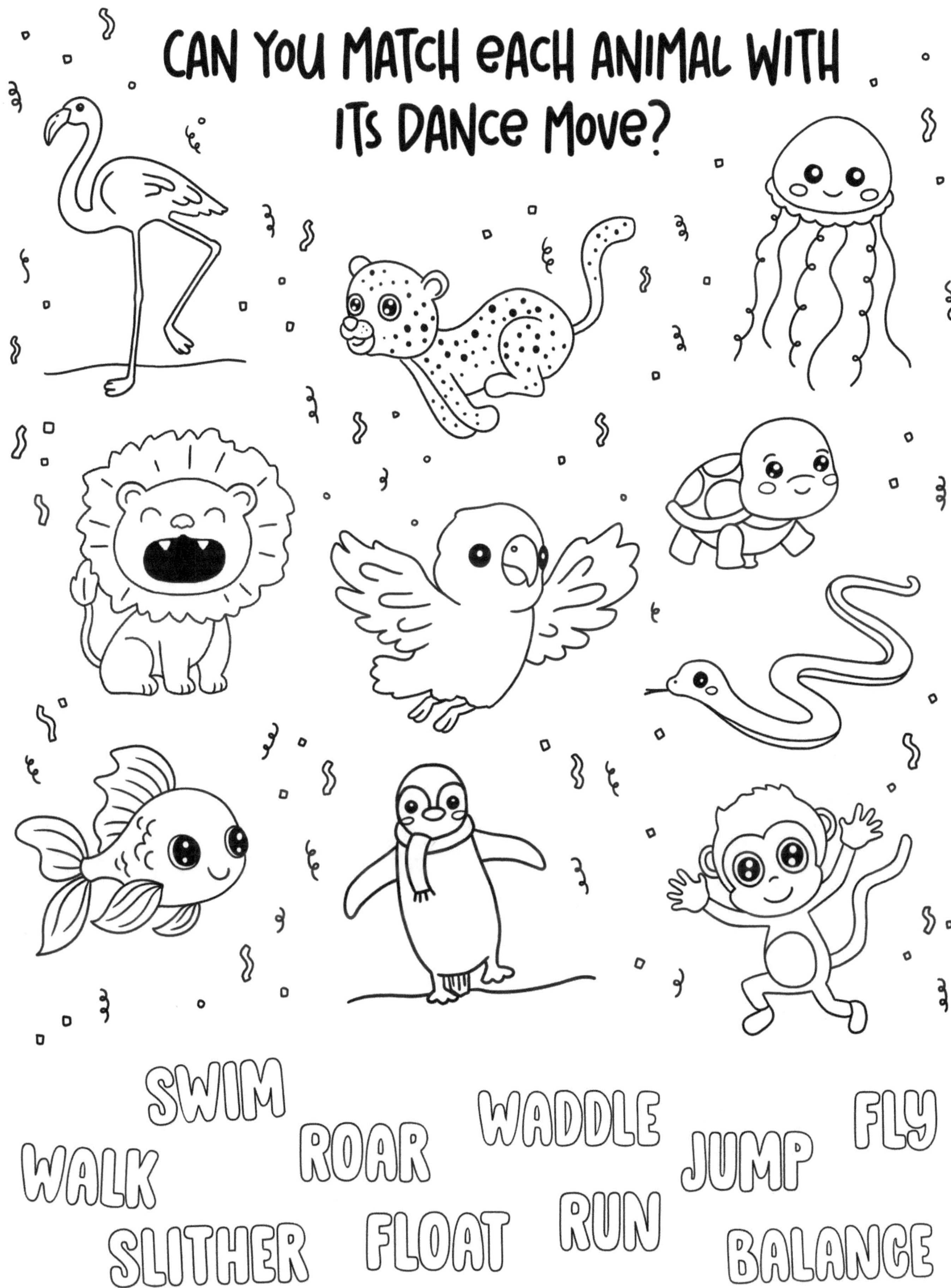

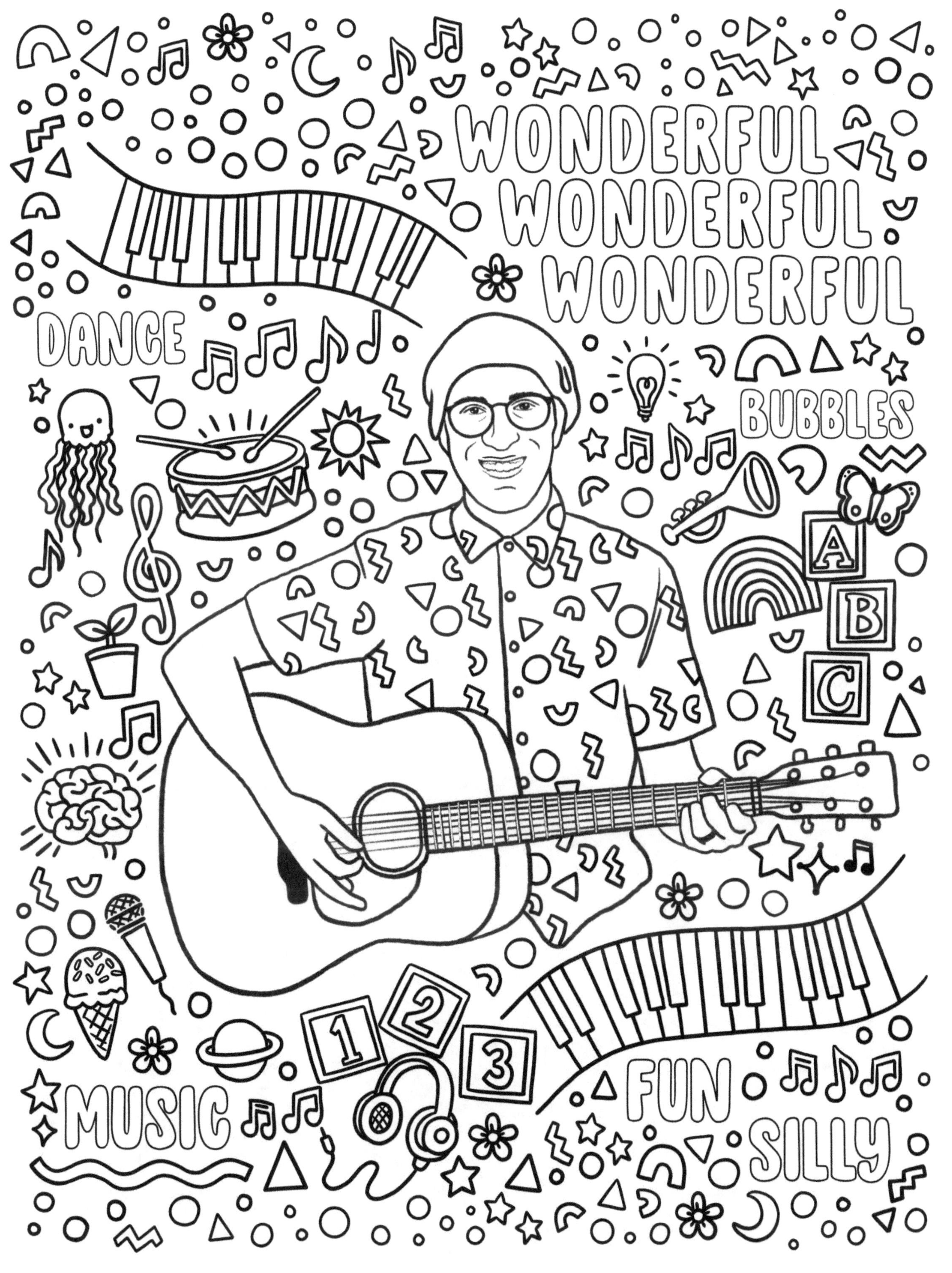
WONDERFUL
WONDERFUL
WONDERFUL
DANCE
BUBBLES
A
B
C
1
2
3
MUSIC
FUN
SILLY

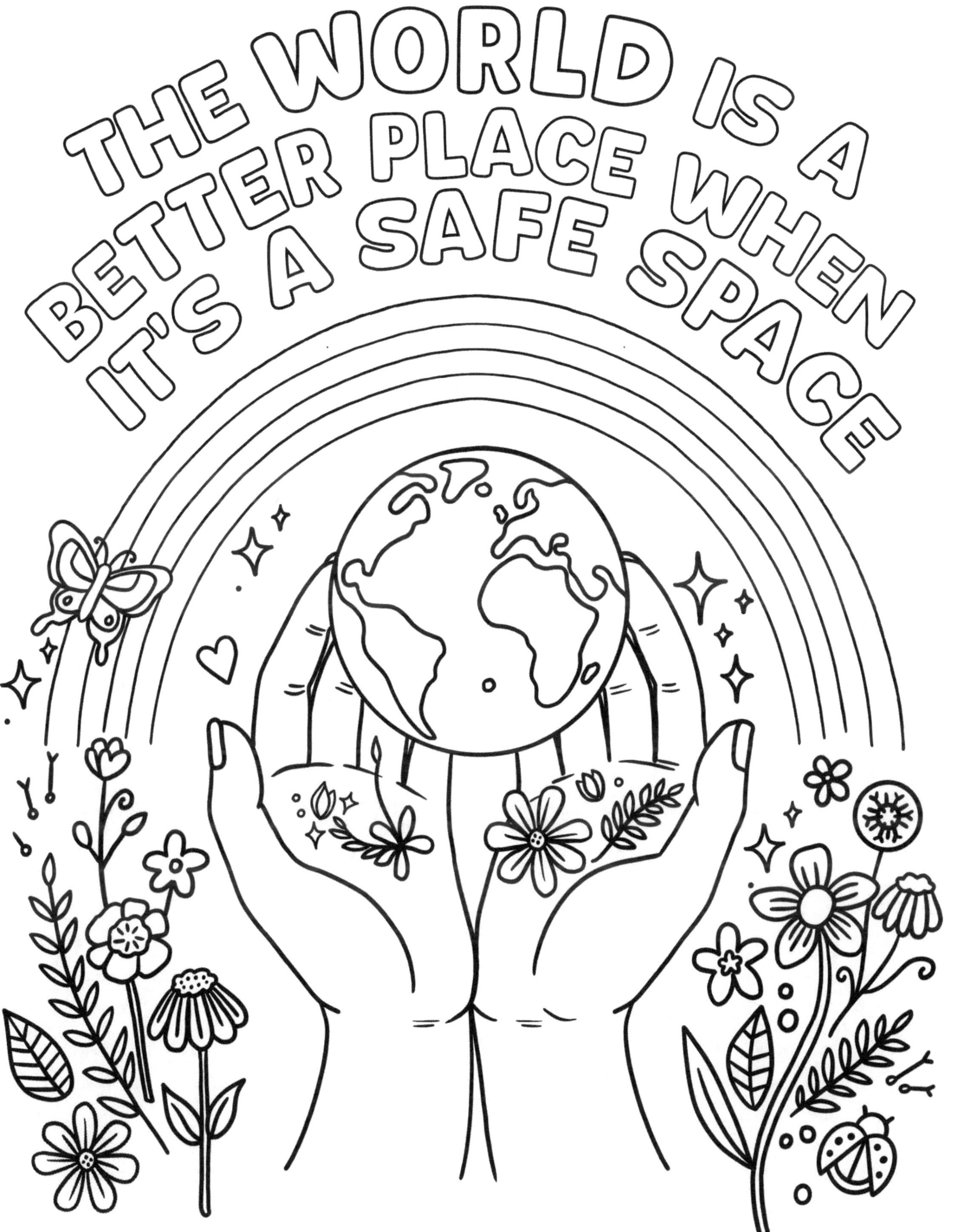
THE WORLD IS A
BETTER PLACE WHEN
IT'S A SAFE SPACE

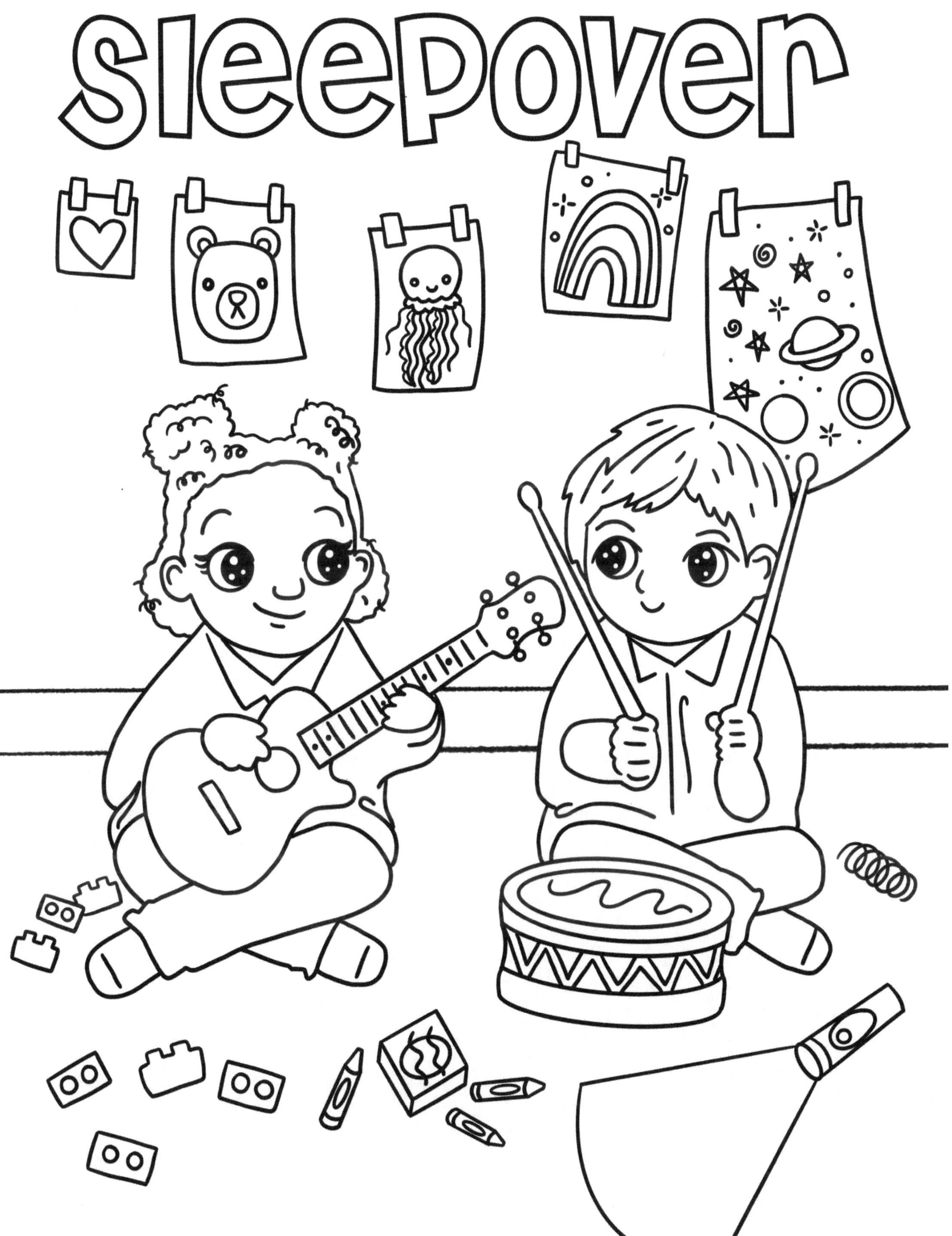
Sleepover

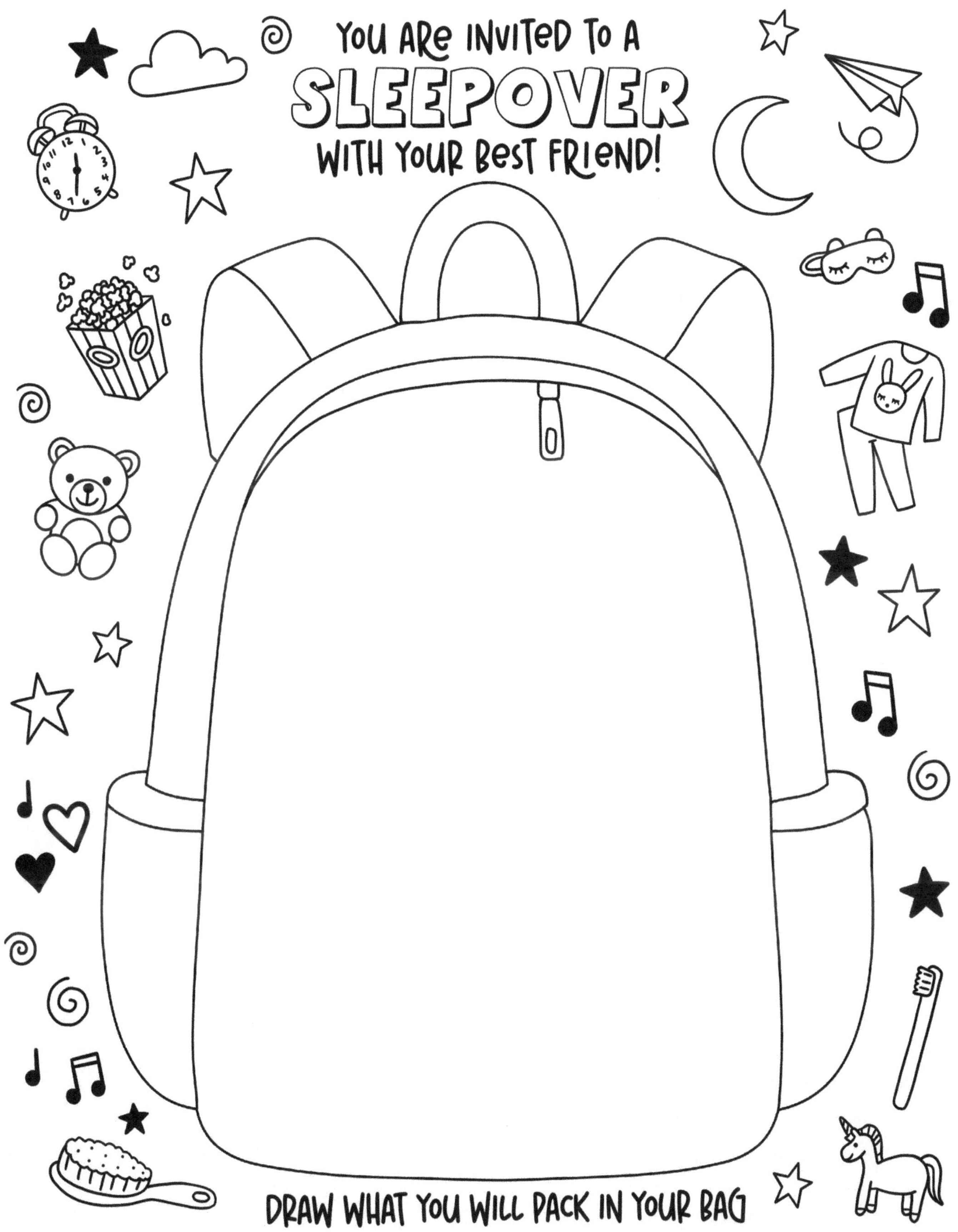

DRAW WHAT YOU WILL PACK IN YOUR BAG

1 2 3 4 5 6 7 8 9 10 NUMBERS

1 2 3 4 5

6 7 8 9 10

11 12 13 14

15 16 17 18

19 20

COUNT TO 20!

Give your brain a big kiss!

Mmmwuaaaaahhhaaa!

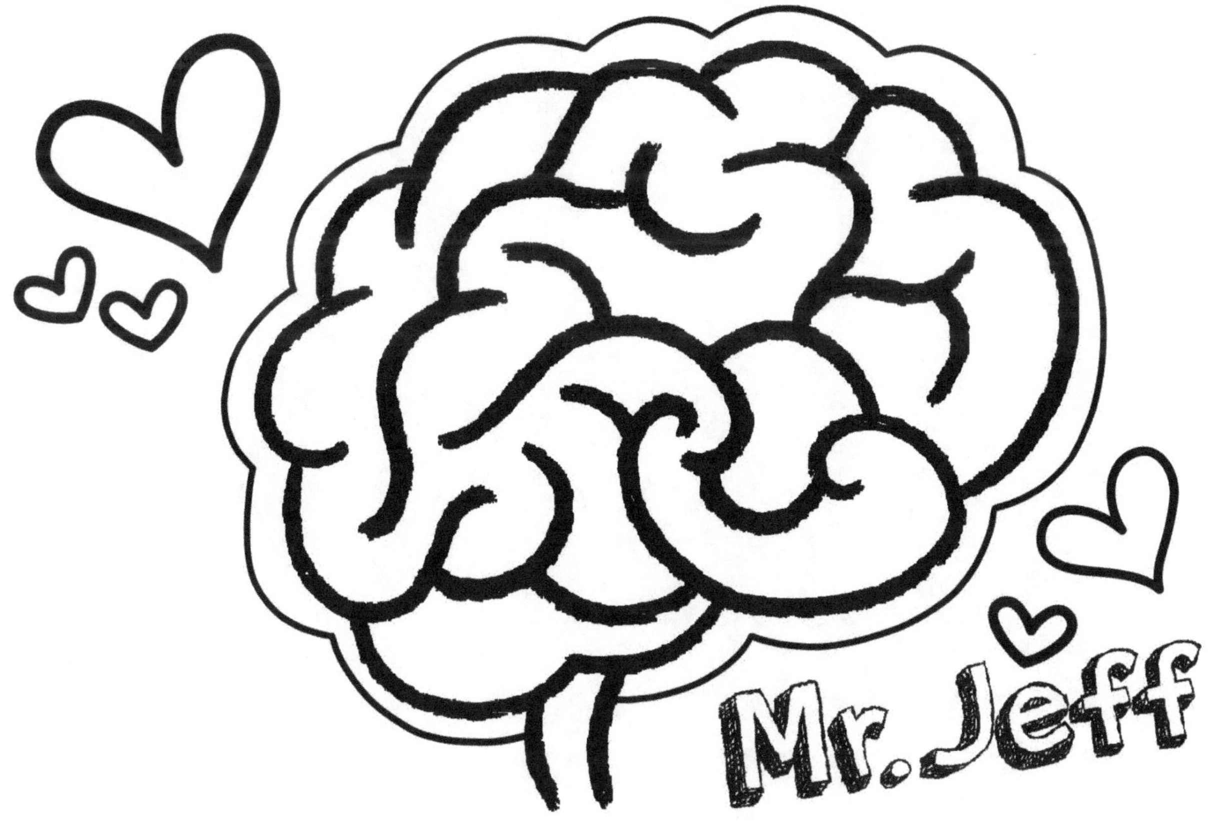

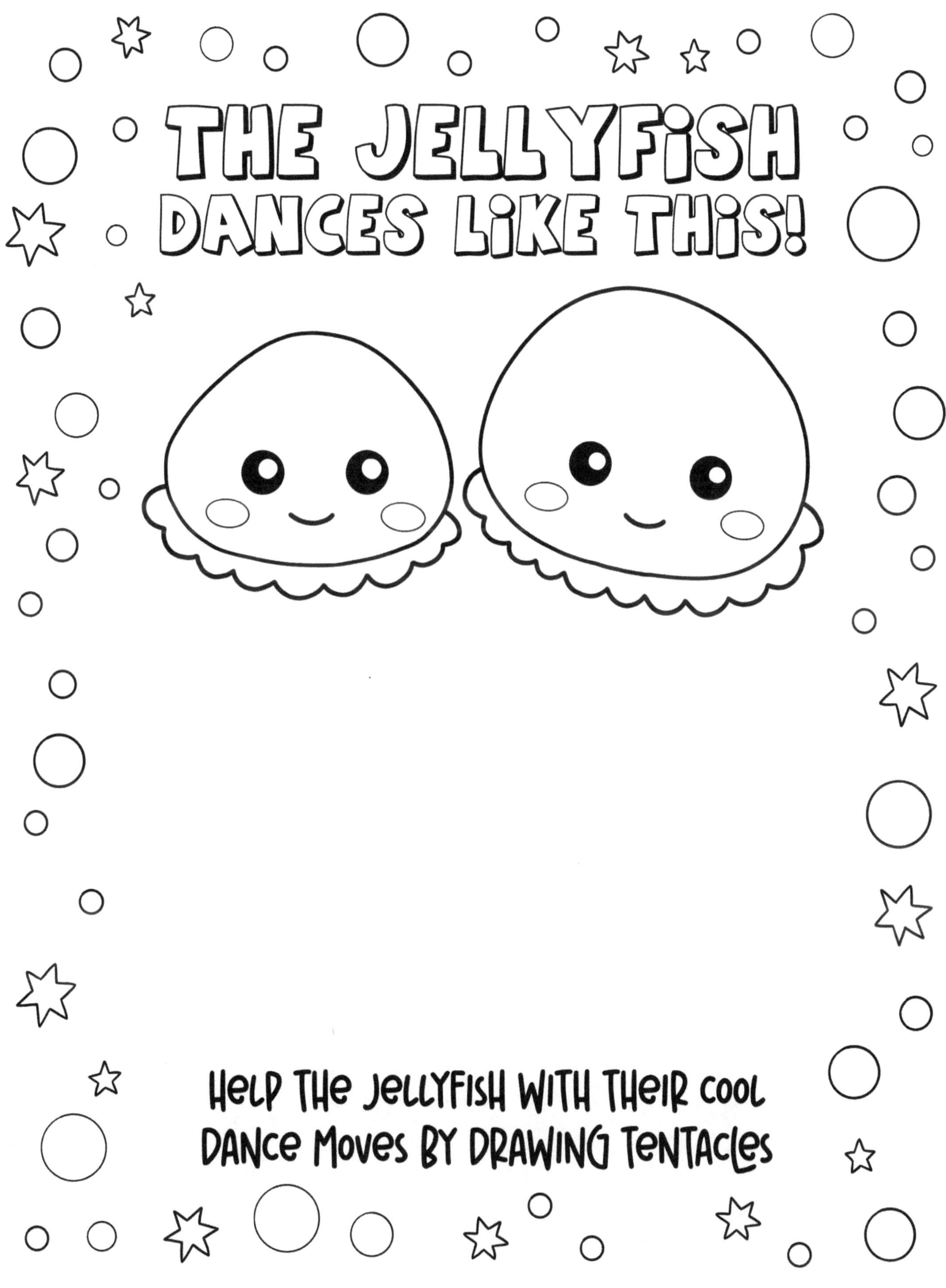
THE JELLYFISH
DANCES LIKE THIS!
HELP THE JELLYFISH WITH THEIR COOL
DANCE MOVES BY DRAWING TENTACLES

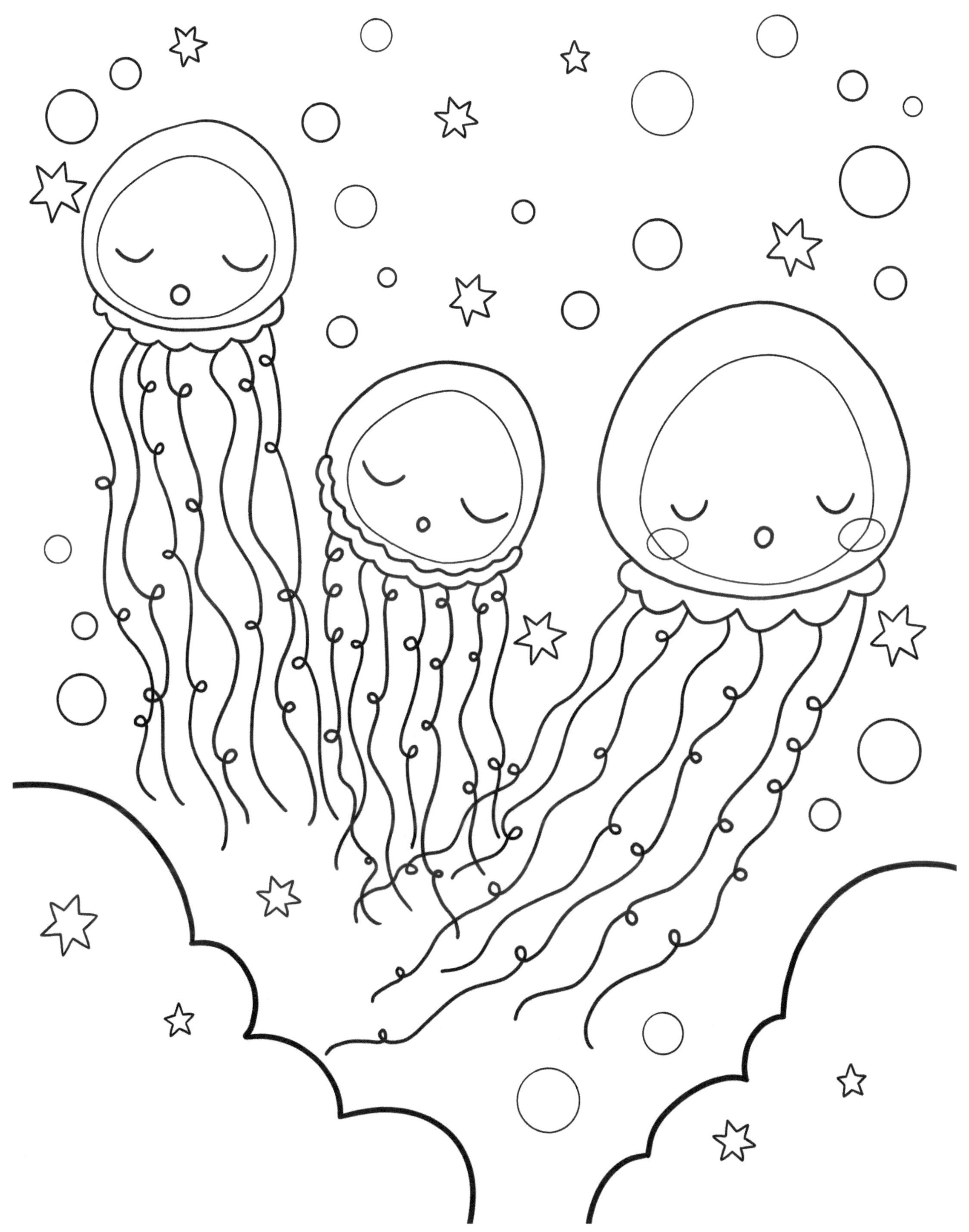

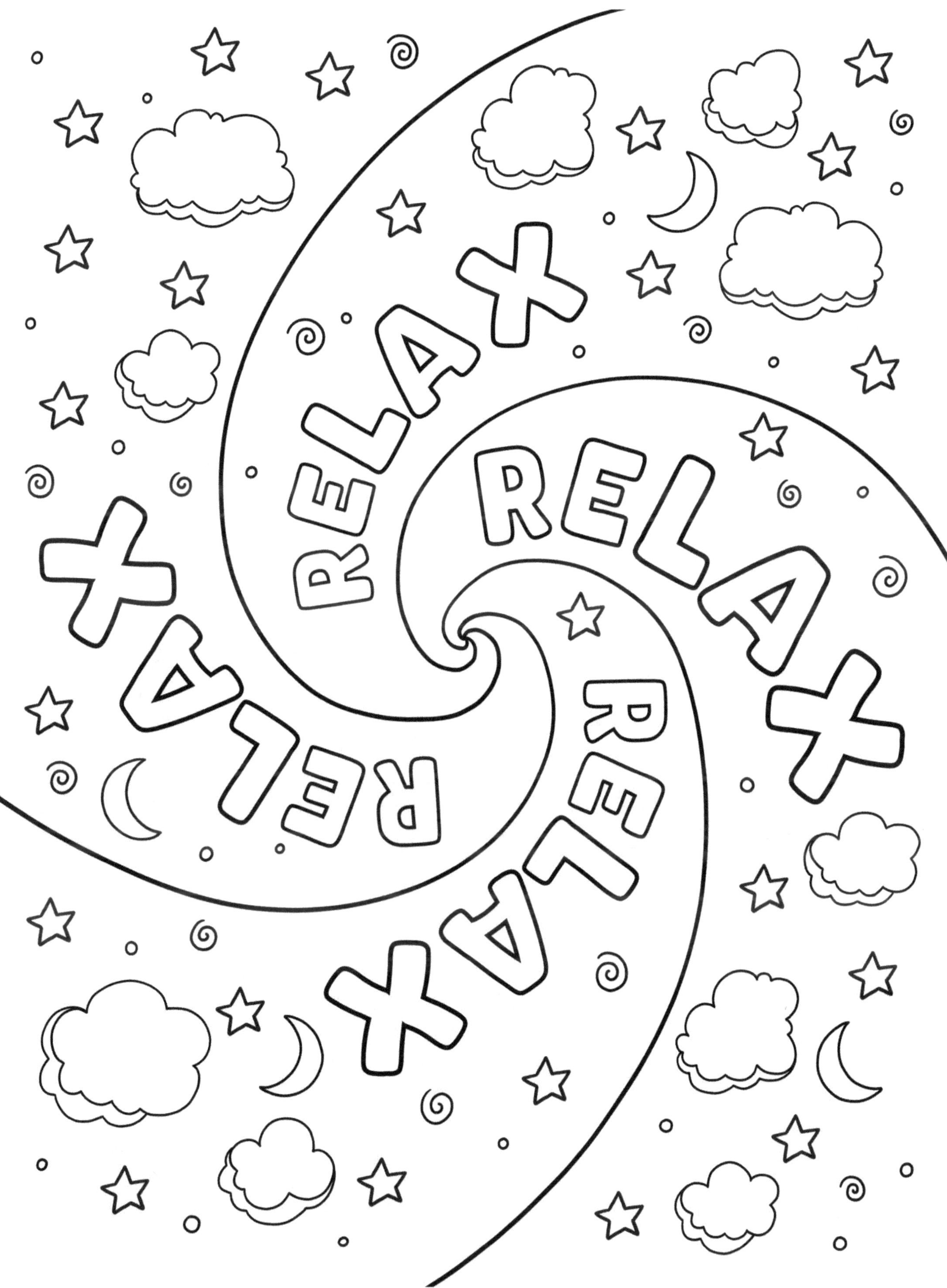
RELAX
RELAX
RELAX
RELAX

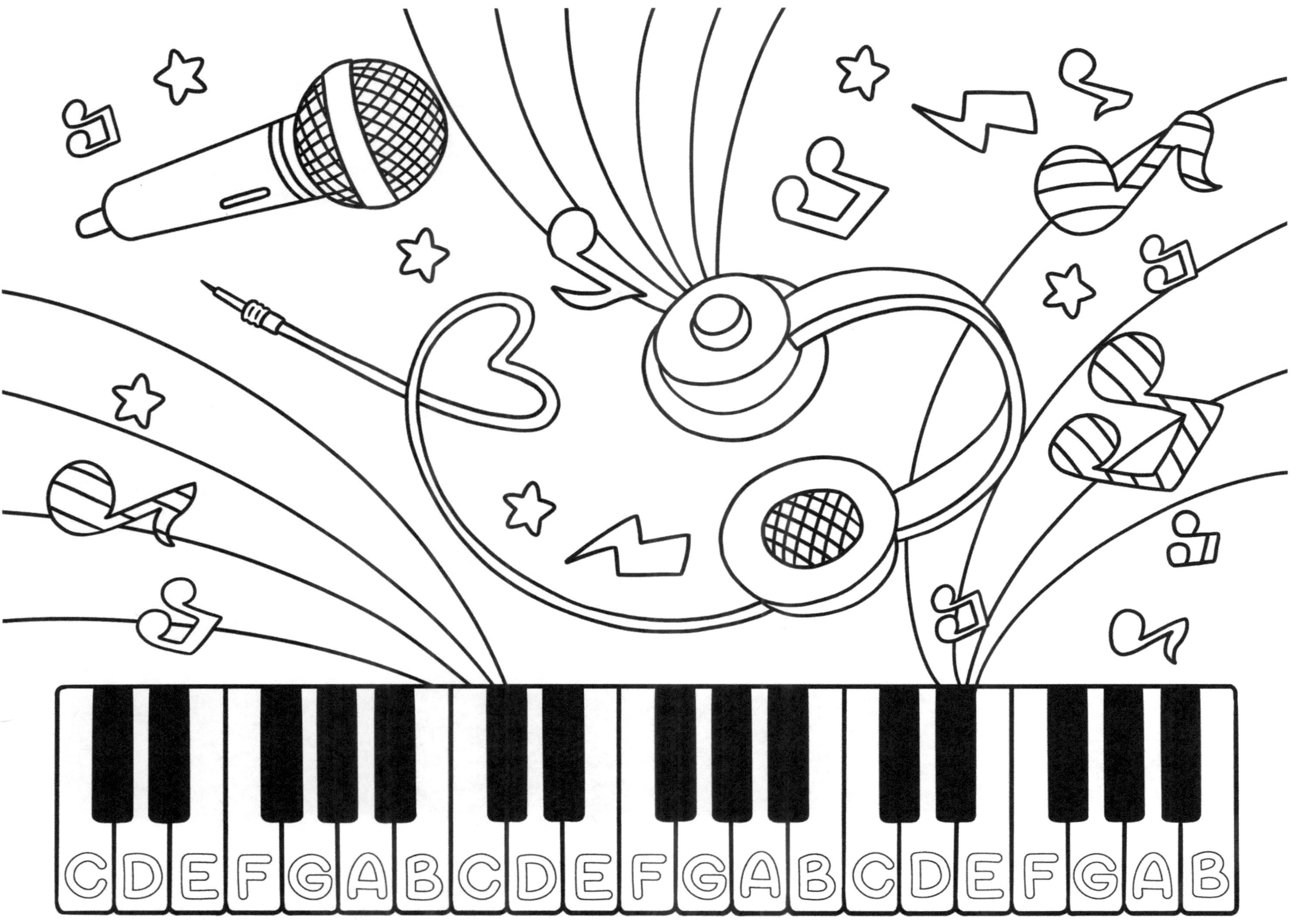
C D E F G A B C D E F G A B C D E F G A B

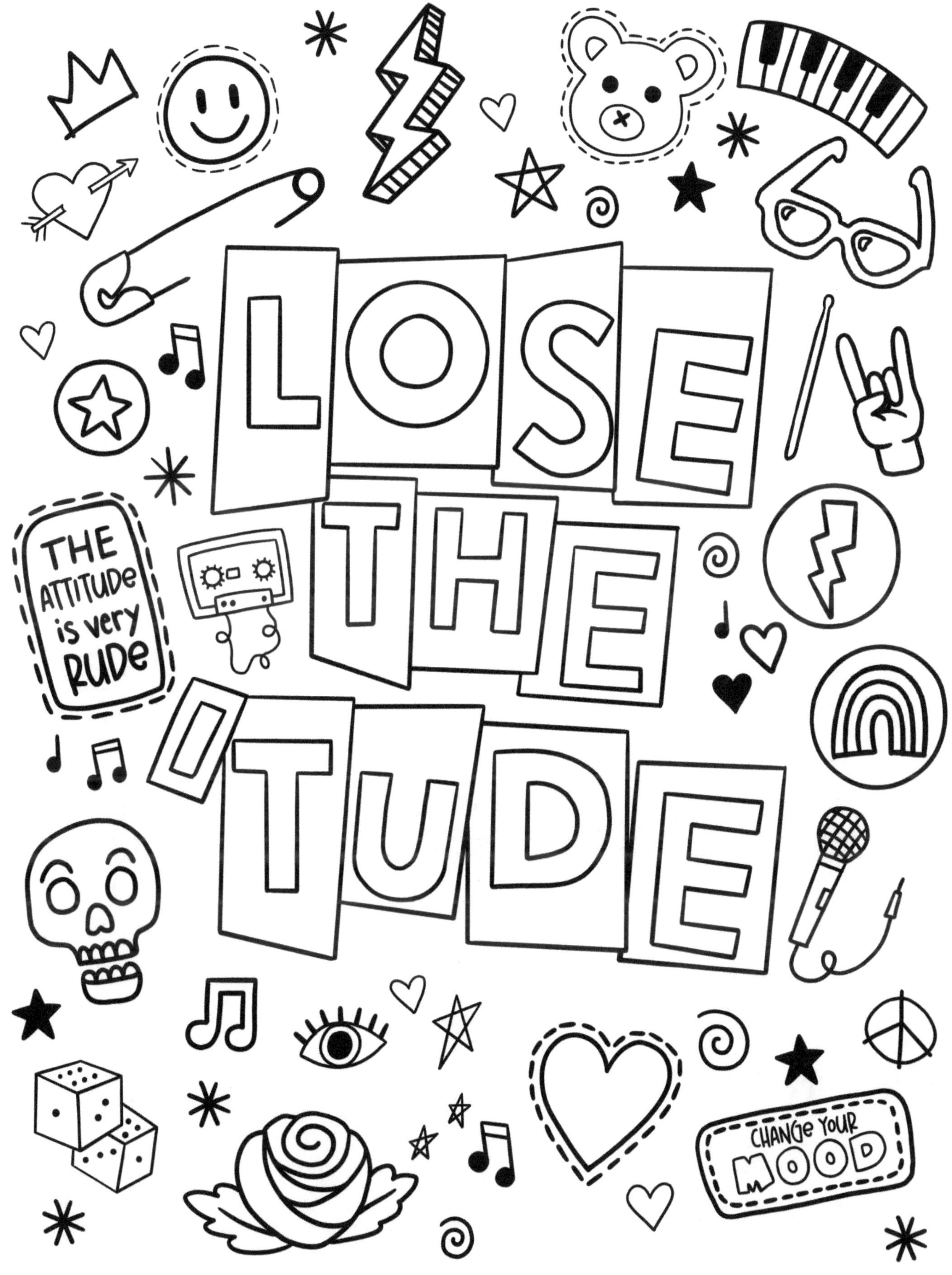
LOSE THE 'TUDE
THE ATTITUDE is very RUDE
CHANGE YOUR MOOD

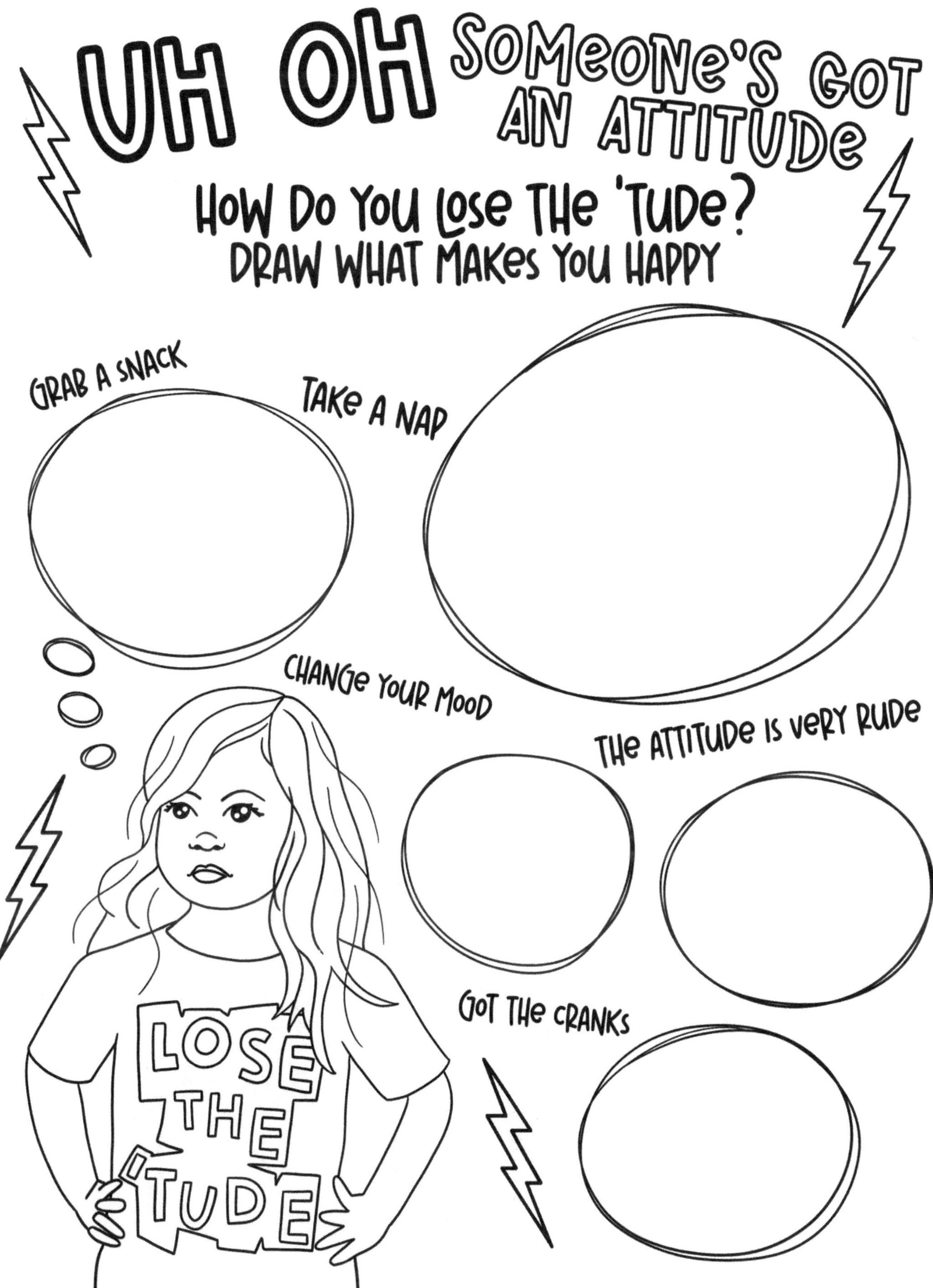
UH OH SOMEONE'S GOT AN ATTITUDE
HOW DO YOU LOSE THE 'TUDE?
DRAW WHAT MAKES YOU HAPPY
GRAB A SNACK
TAKE A NAP
CHANGE YOUR MOOD
THE ATTITUDE IS VERY RUDE
GOT THE CRANKS
LOSE THE 'TUDE

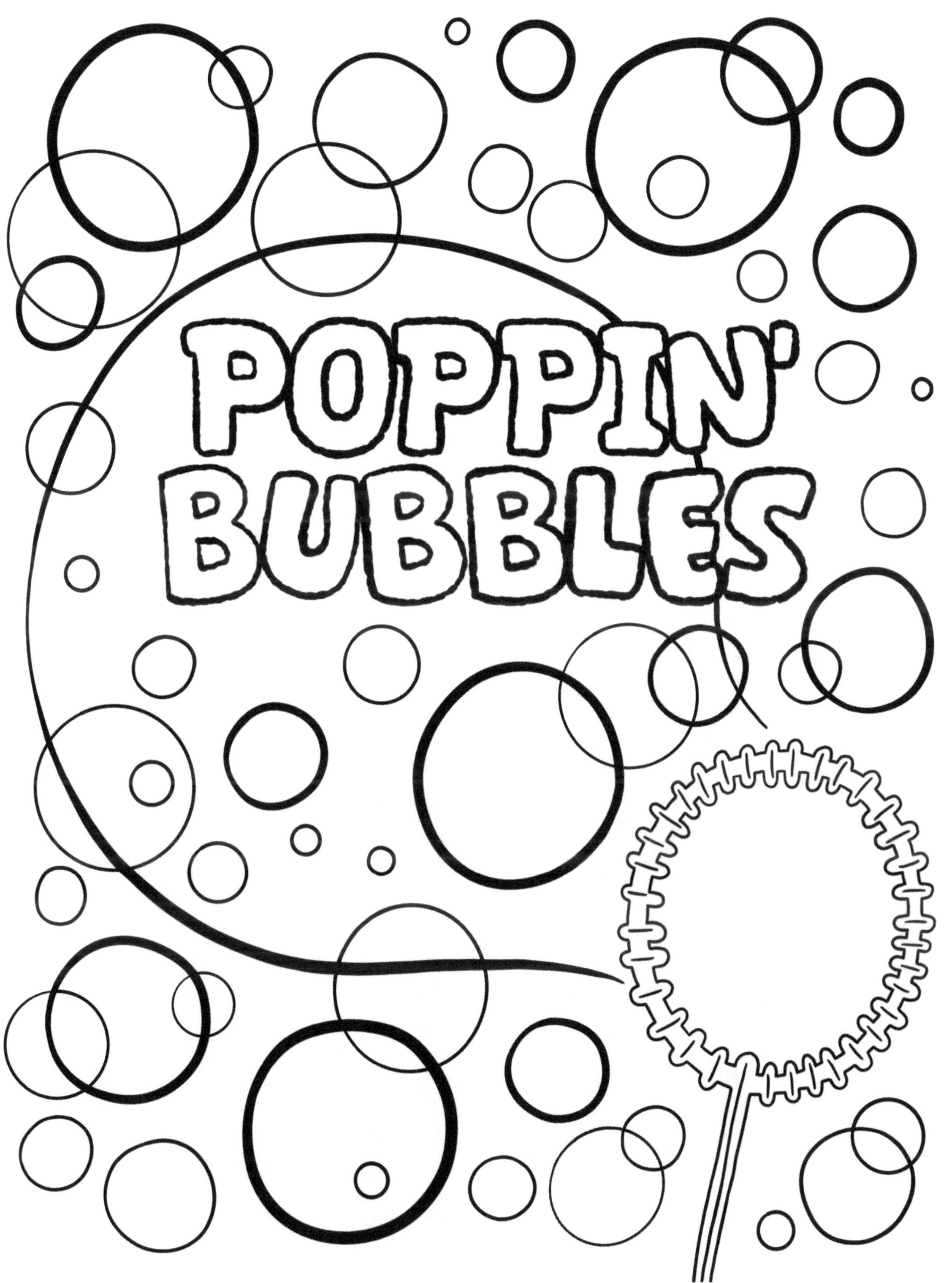
POPPIN'
BUBBLES

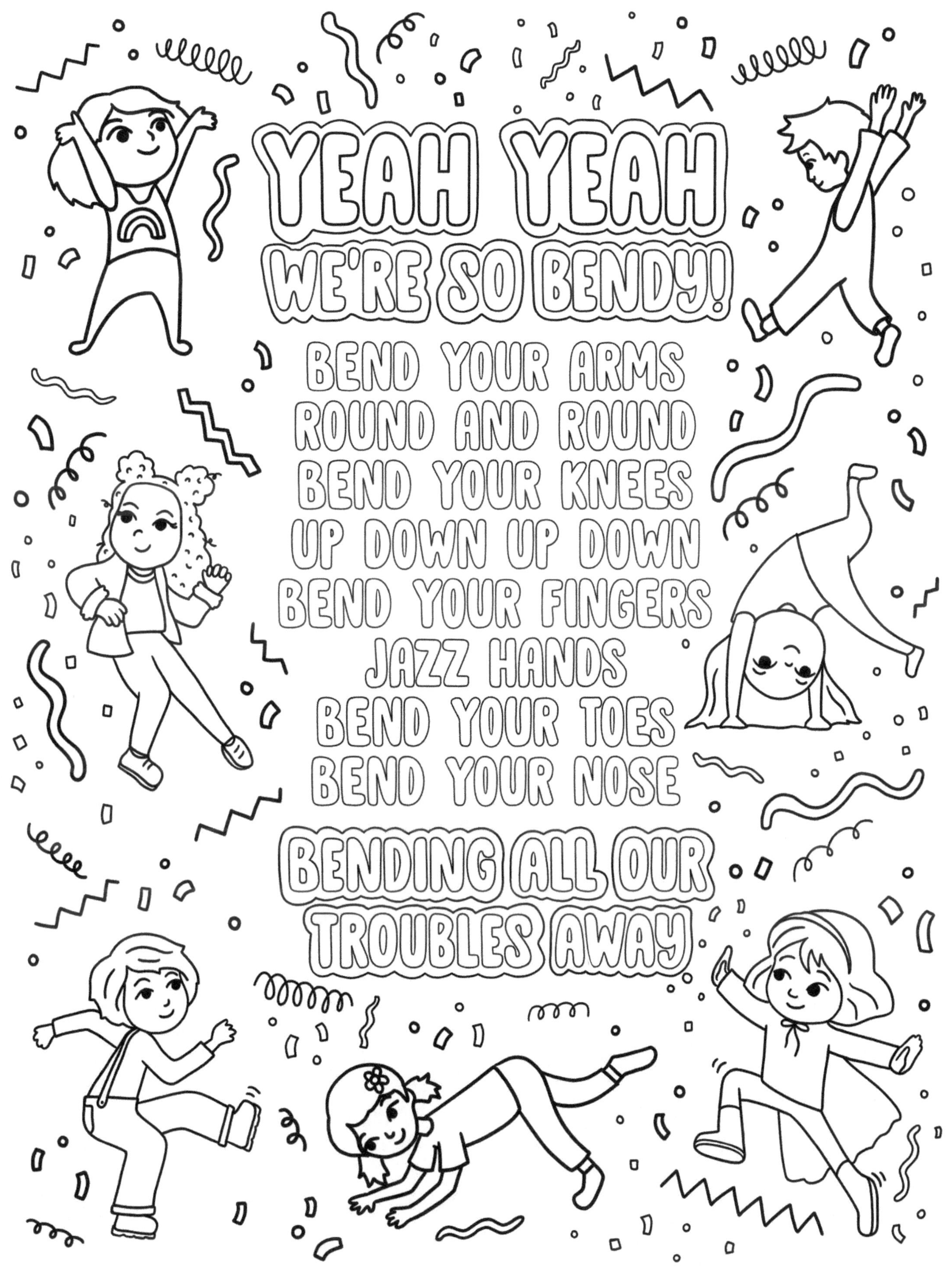
YEAH YEAH
WE'RE SO BENDY!
BEND YOUR ARMS
ROUND AND ROUND
BEND YOUR KNEES
UP DOWN UP DOWN
BEND YOUR FINGERS
JAZZ HANDS
BEND YOUR TOES
BEND YOUR NOSE
BENDING ALL OUR
TROUBLES AWAY

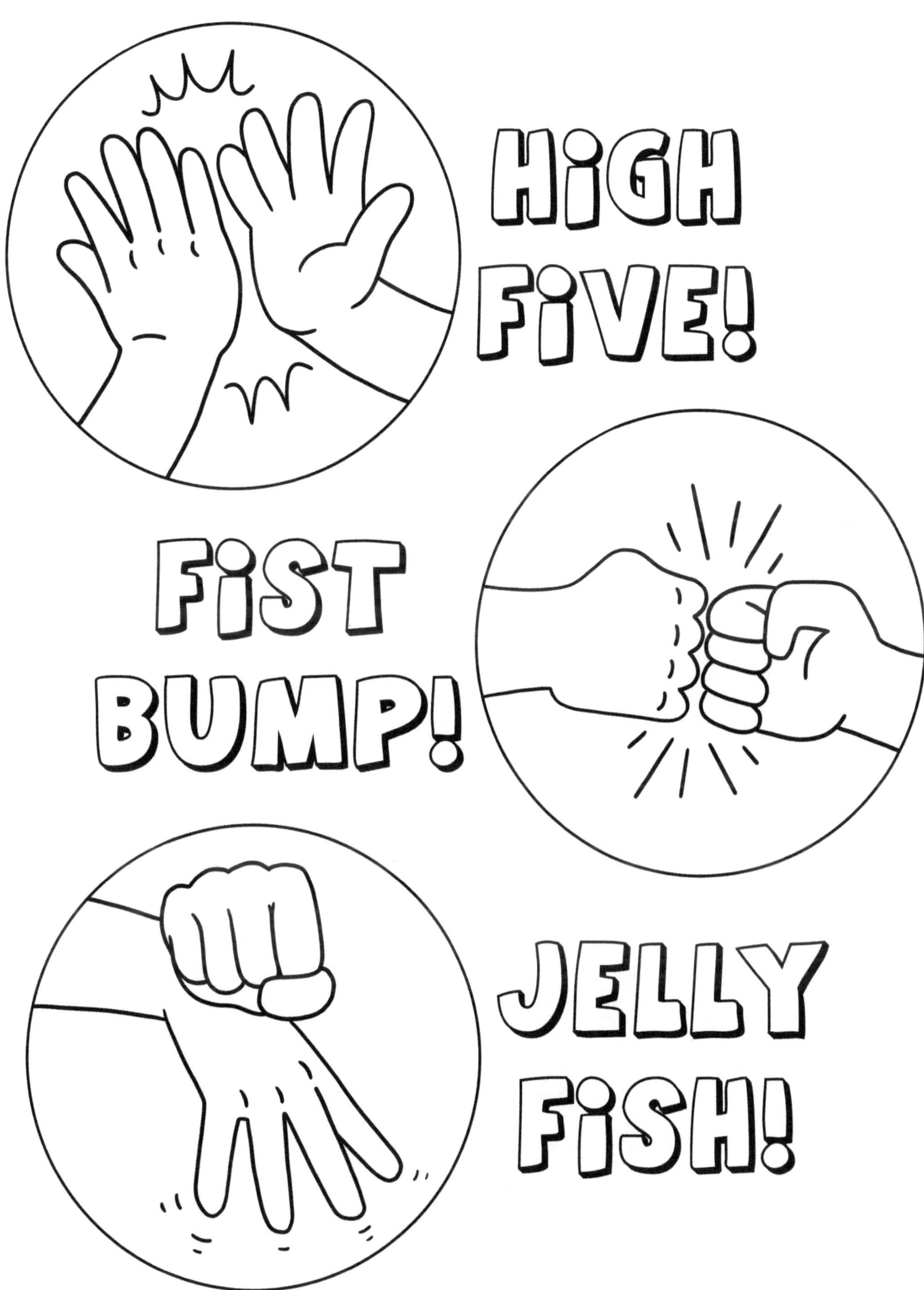
HIGH
FIVE!
FIST
BUMP!
JELLY
FISH!

GIVE ME A HIGH FIVE!
TRACE YOUR HAND HERE

IT IS YOUR BIRTHDAY.

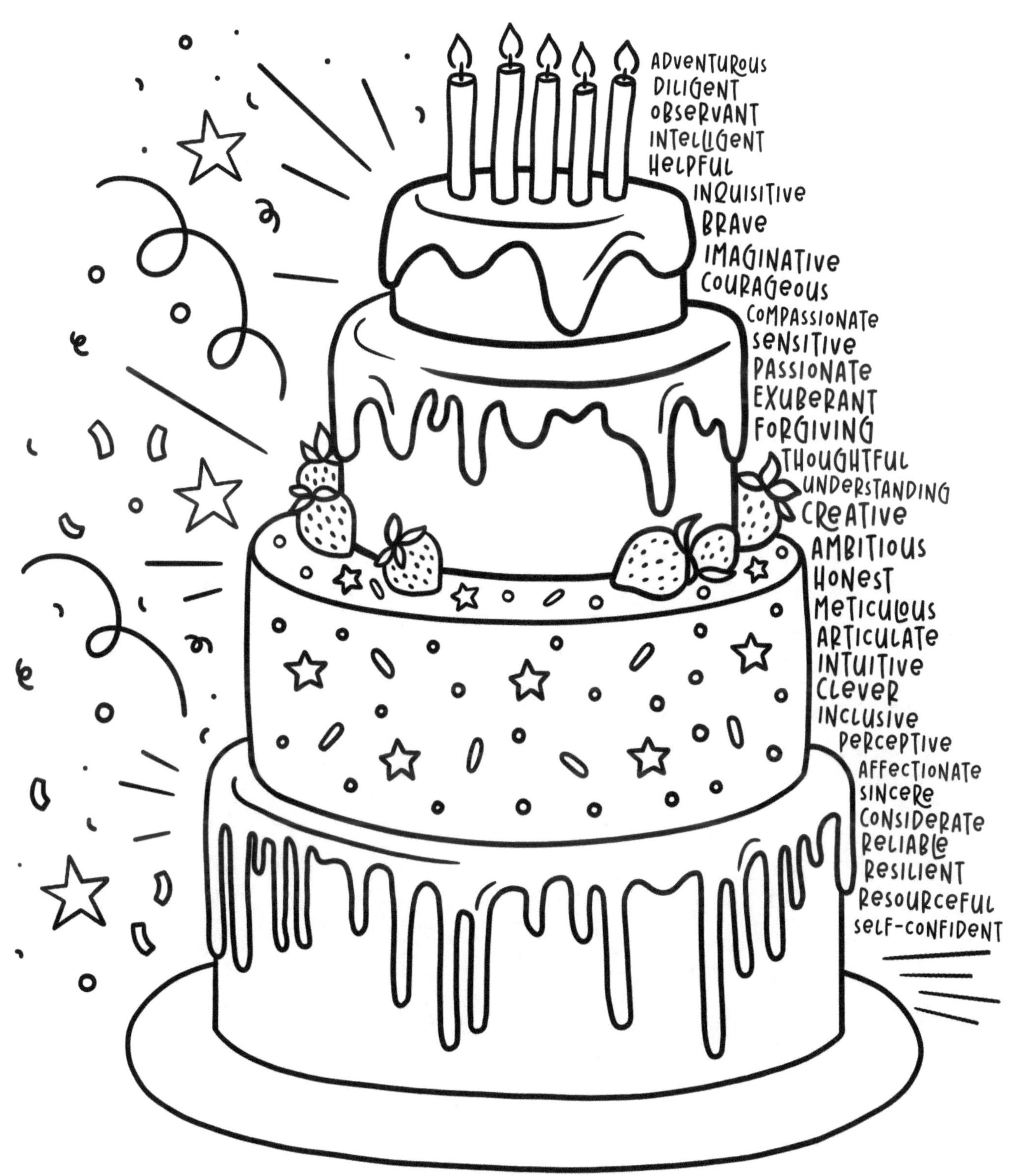

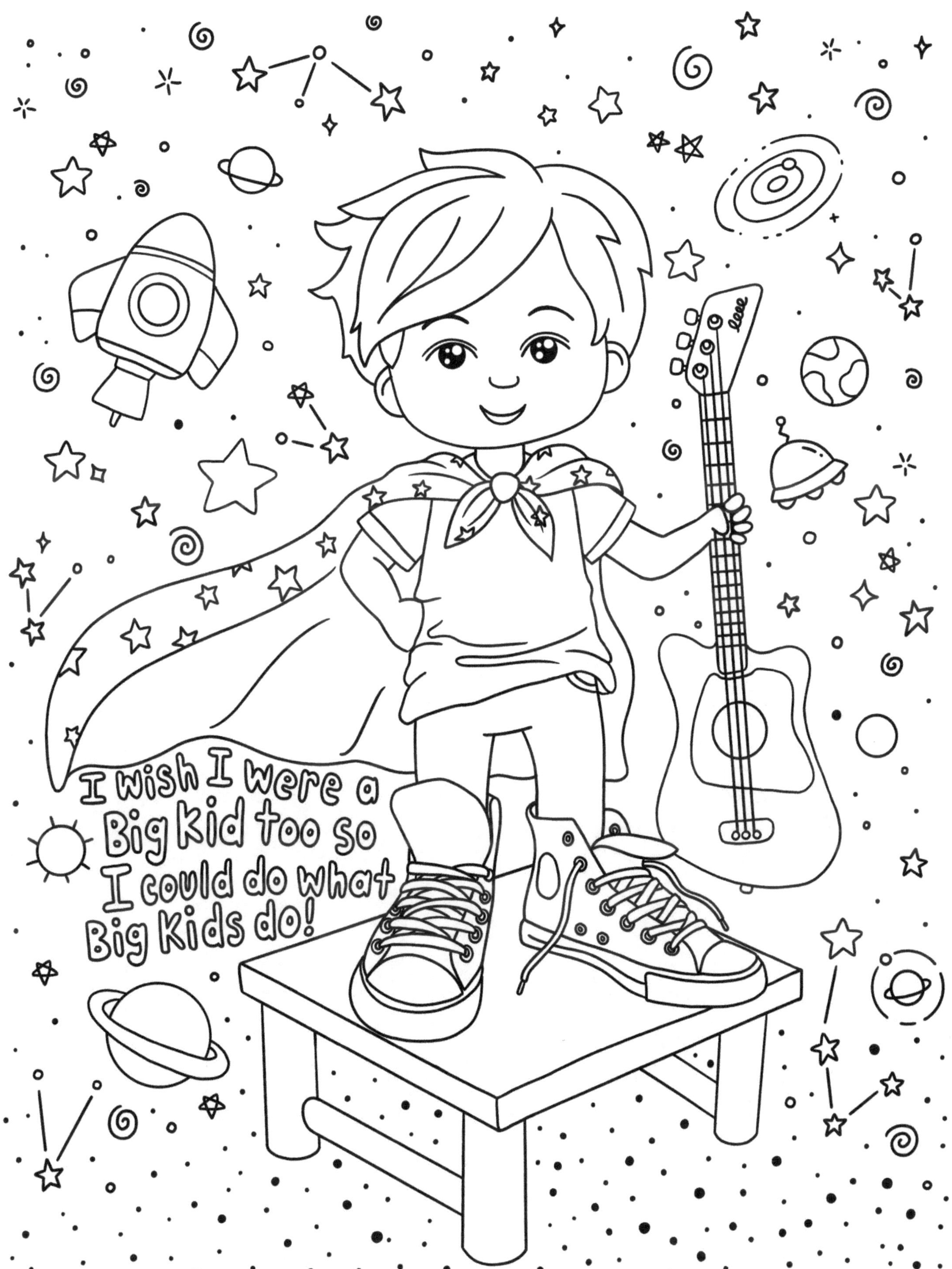
I wish I were a
Big Kid too so
I could do what
Big Kids do!

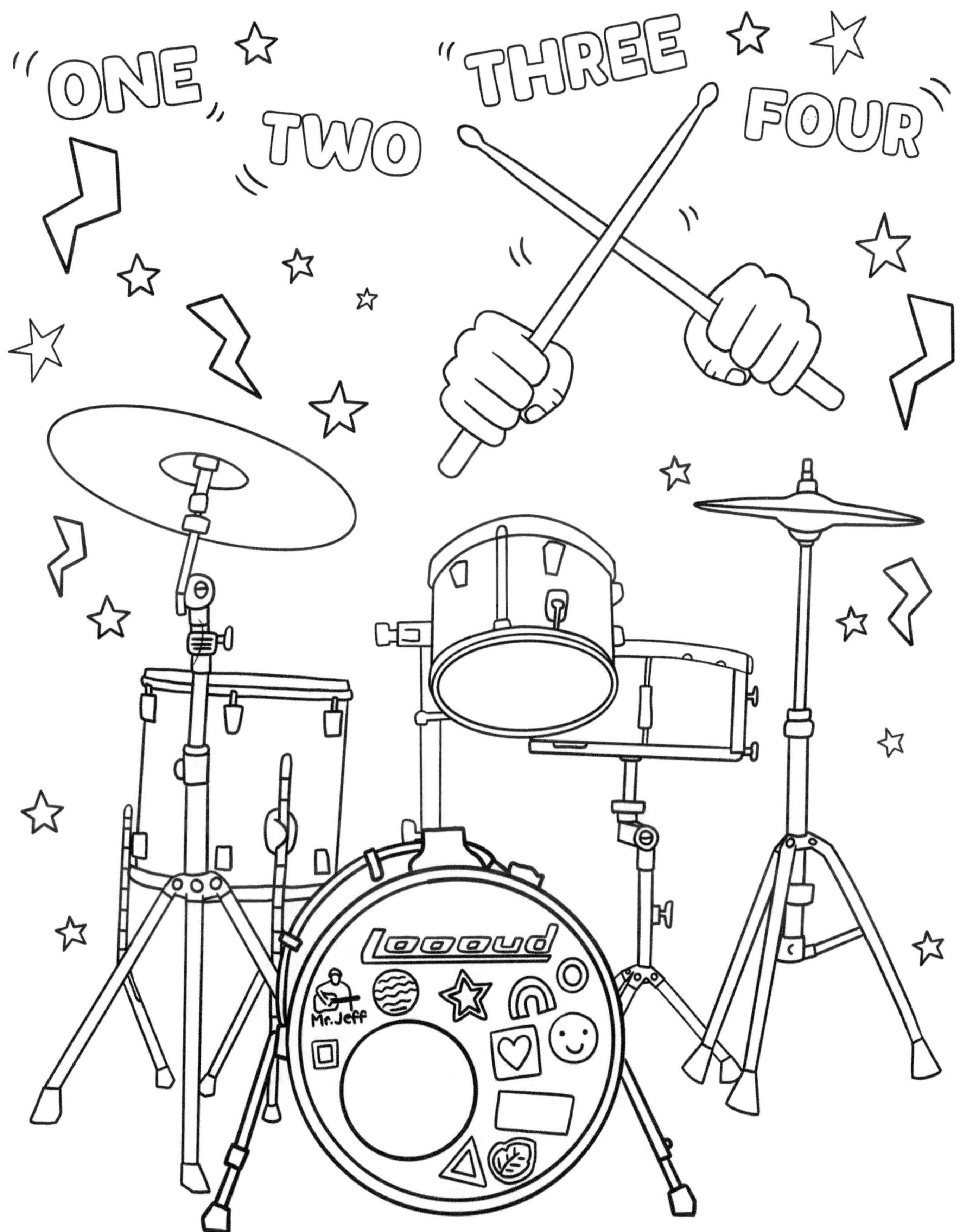
ONE
TWO
THREE
FOUR
Loooud
Mr.Jeff

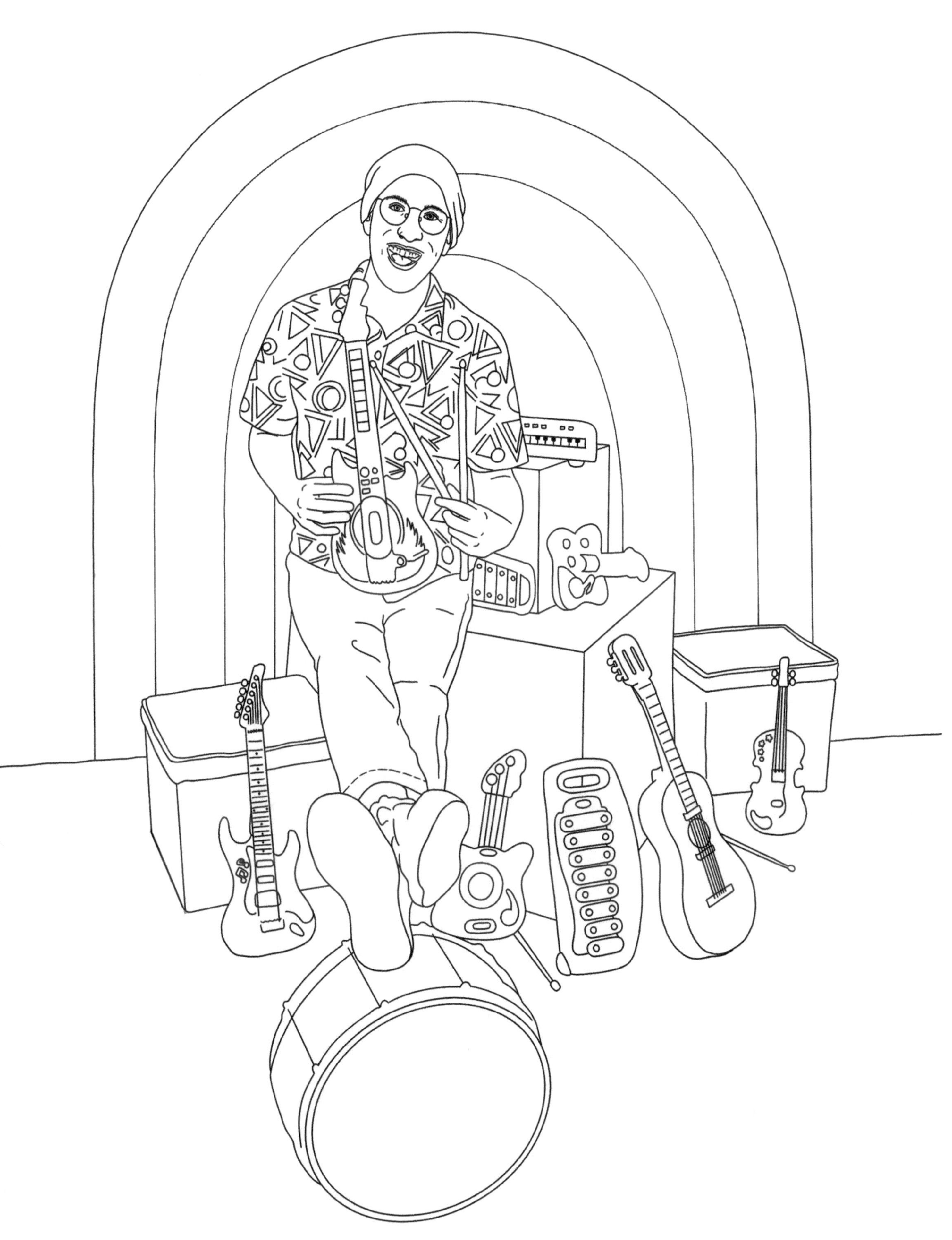

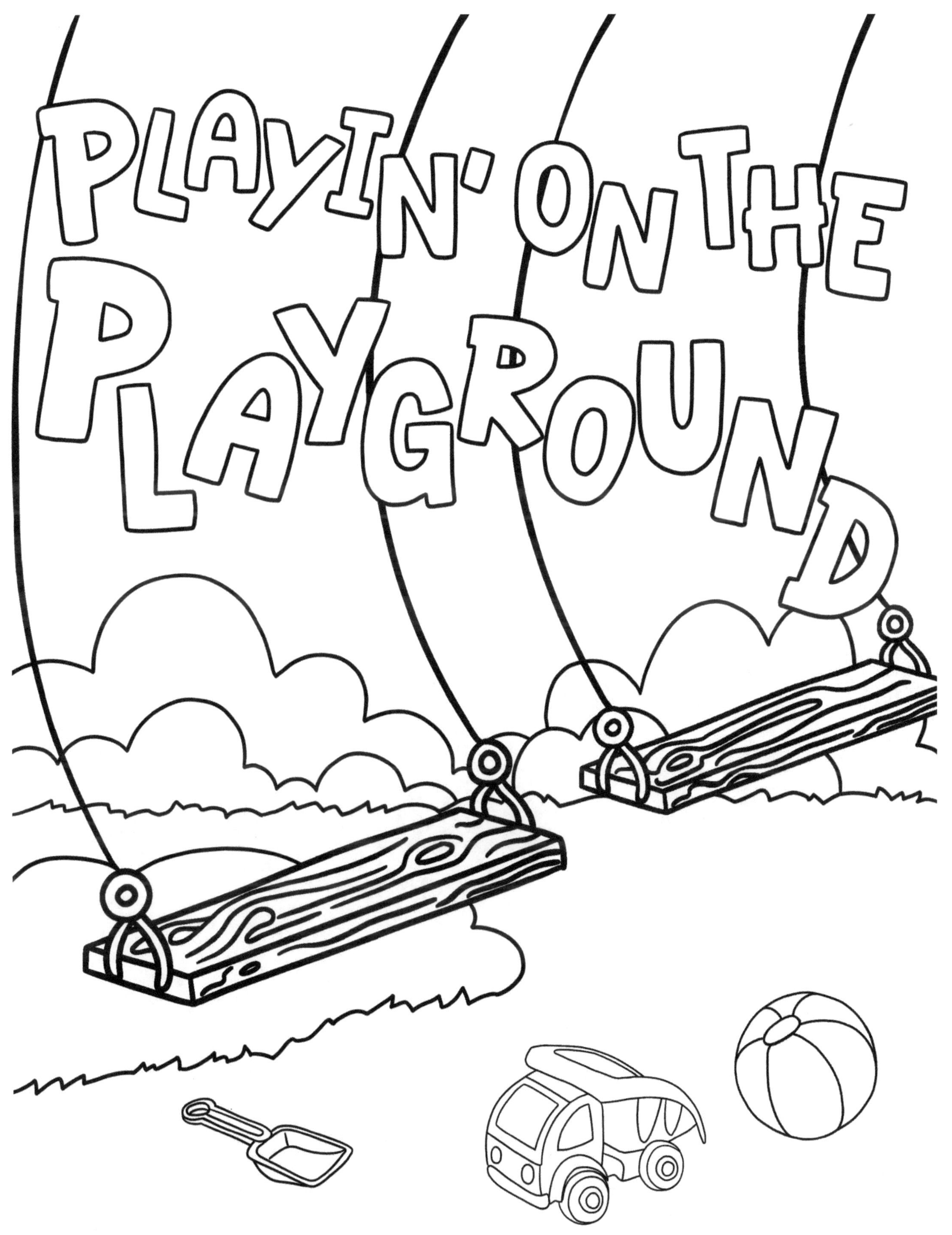
PLAYIN' ON THE
PLAYGROUND

MR. JEFF
LOUD IN THE LIBRARY
STARS
Z
123
456
789

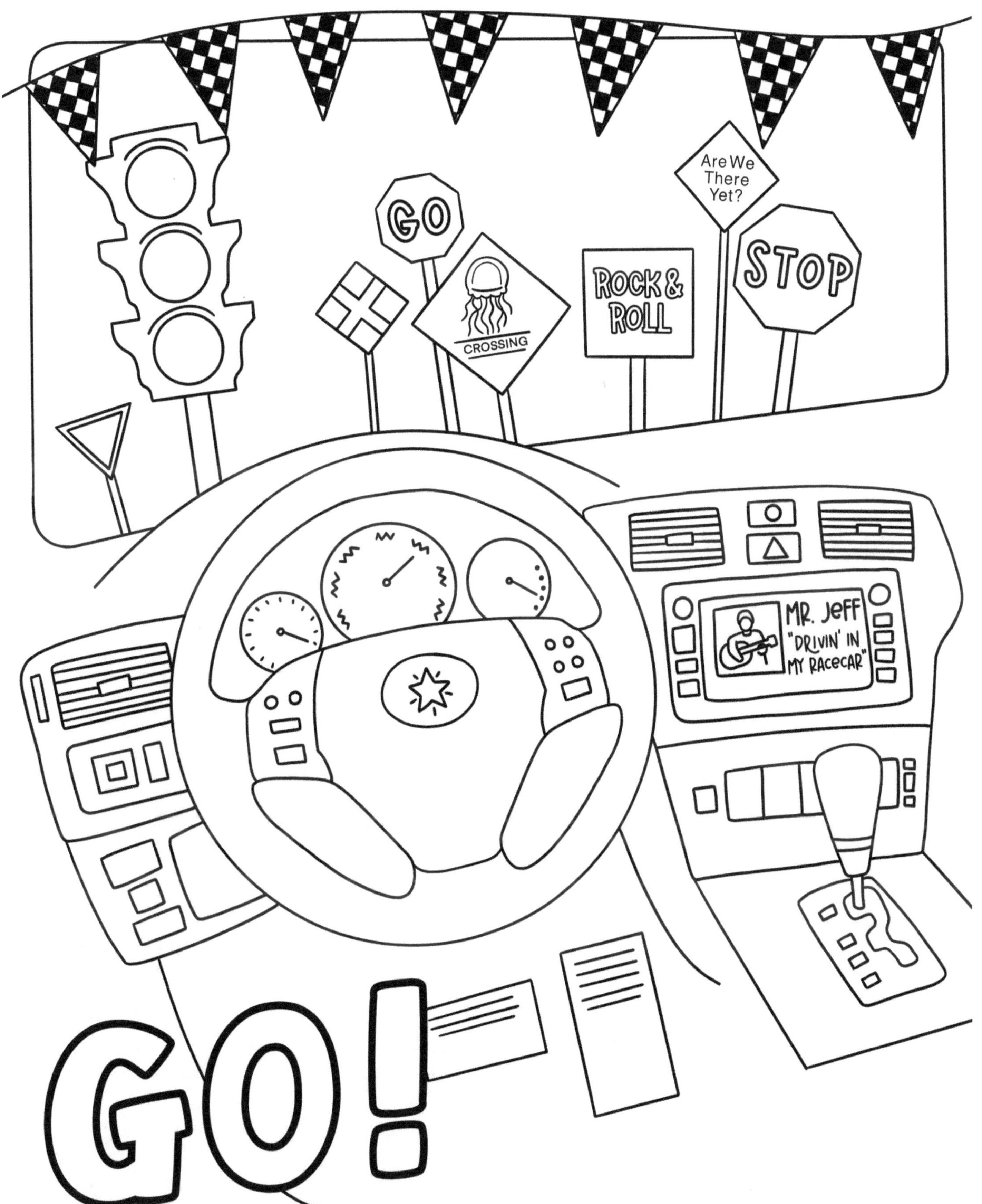
Are We There Yet?
GO
ROCK & ROLL
STOP
CROSSING
MR. JEFF
"DRIVIN' IN MY RACECAR"
GO!

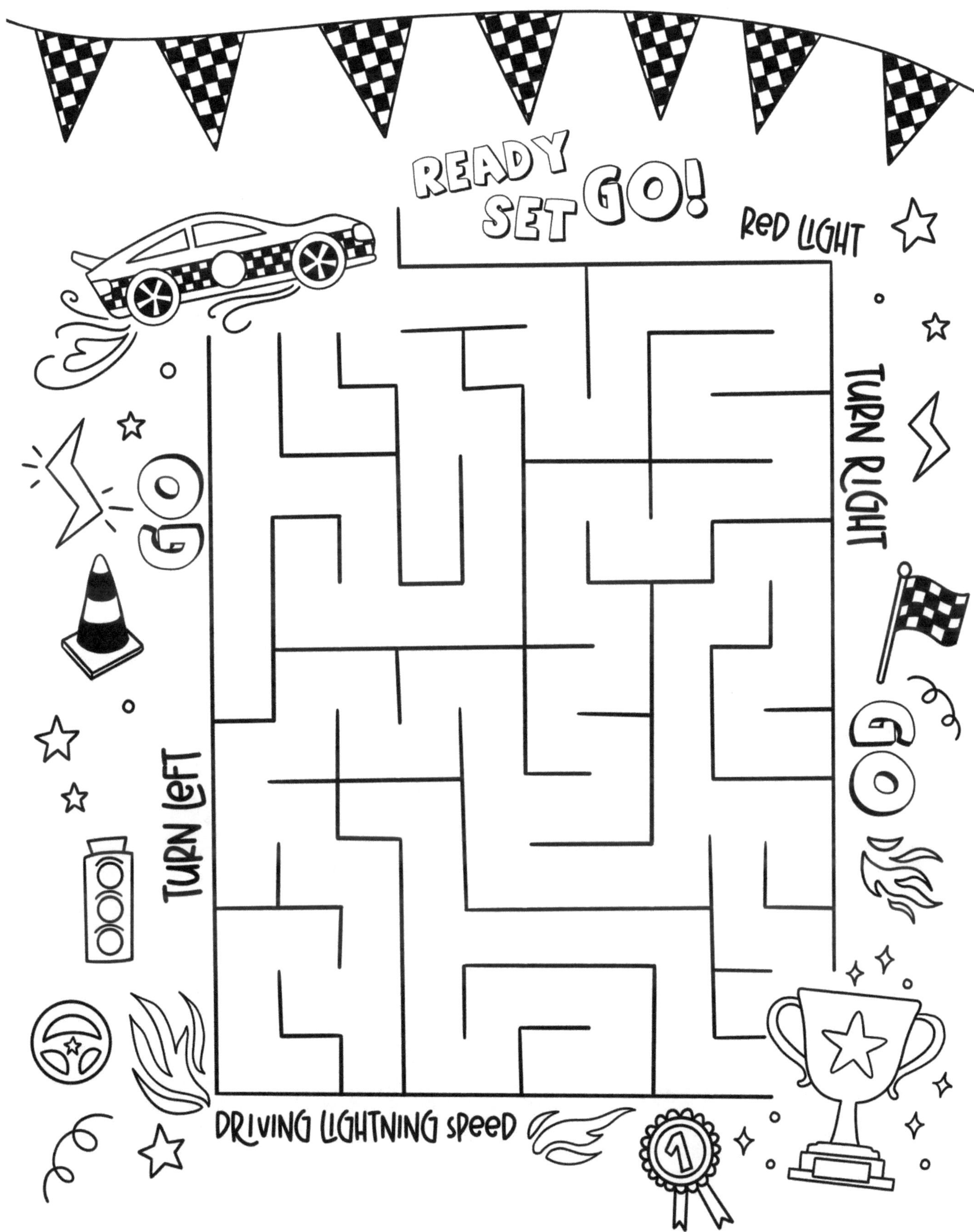

READY
SET GO!
RED LIGHT
GO
TURN RIGHT
GO
TURN LEFT
DRIVING LIGHTNING SPEED
1

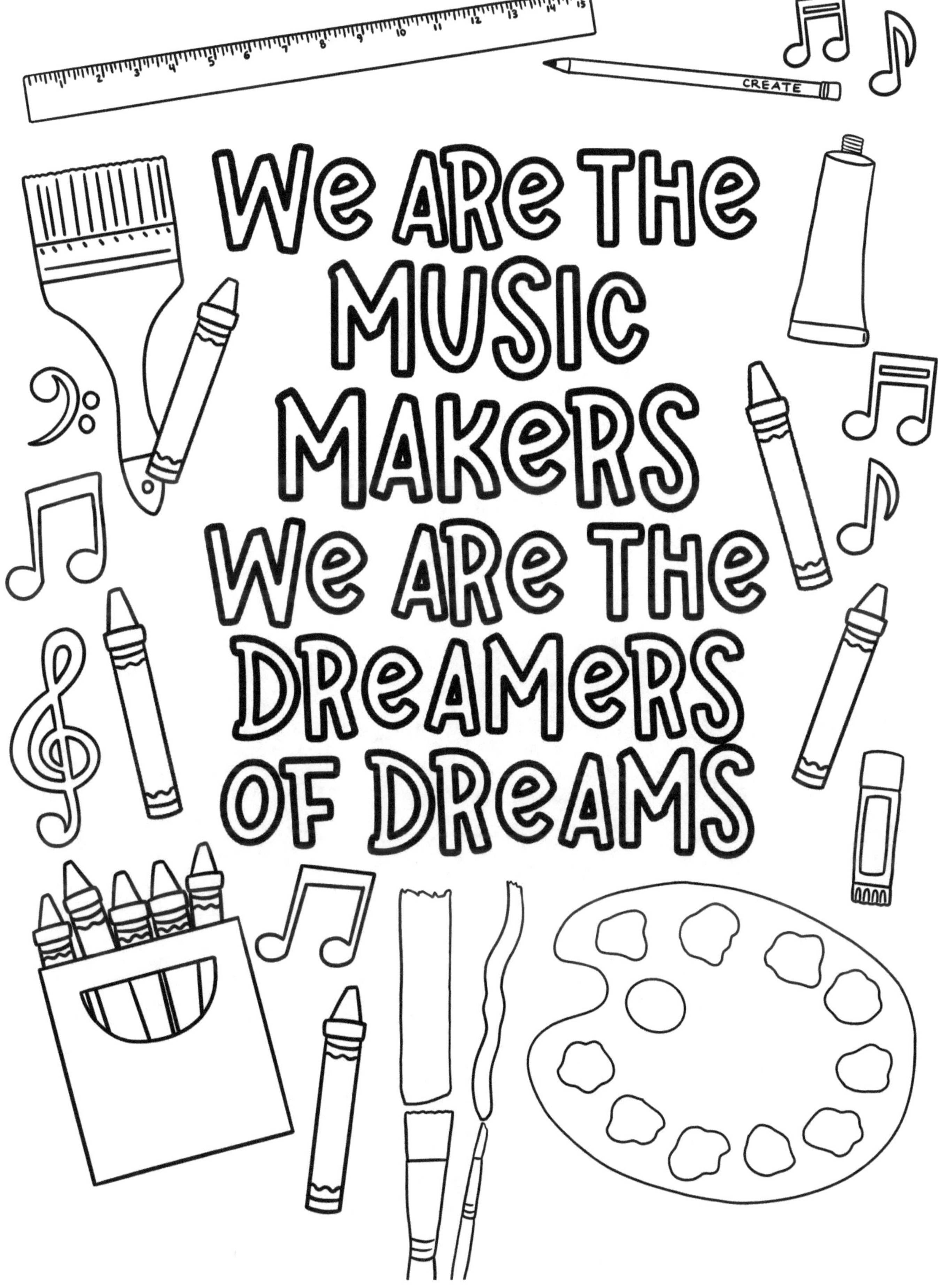
CREATE
WE ARE THE
MUSIC
MAKERS
WE ARE THE
DREAMERS
OF DREAMS

YOU CAN MAKE WHAT YOU WANT TO MAKE
YOU CAN DRAW WHAT YOU WANT TO DRAW

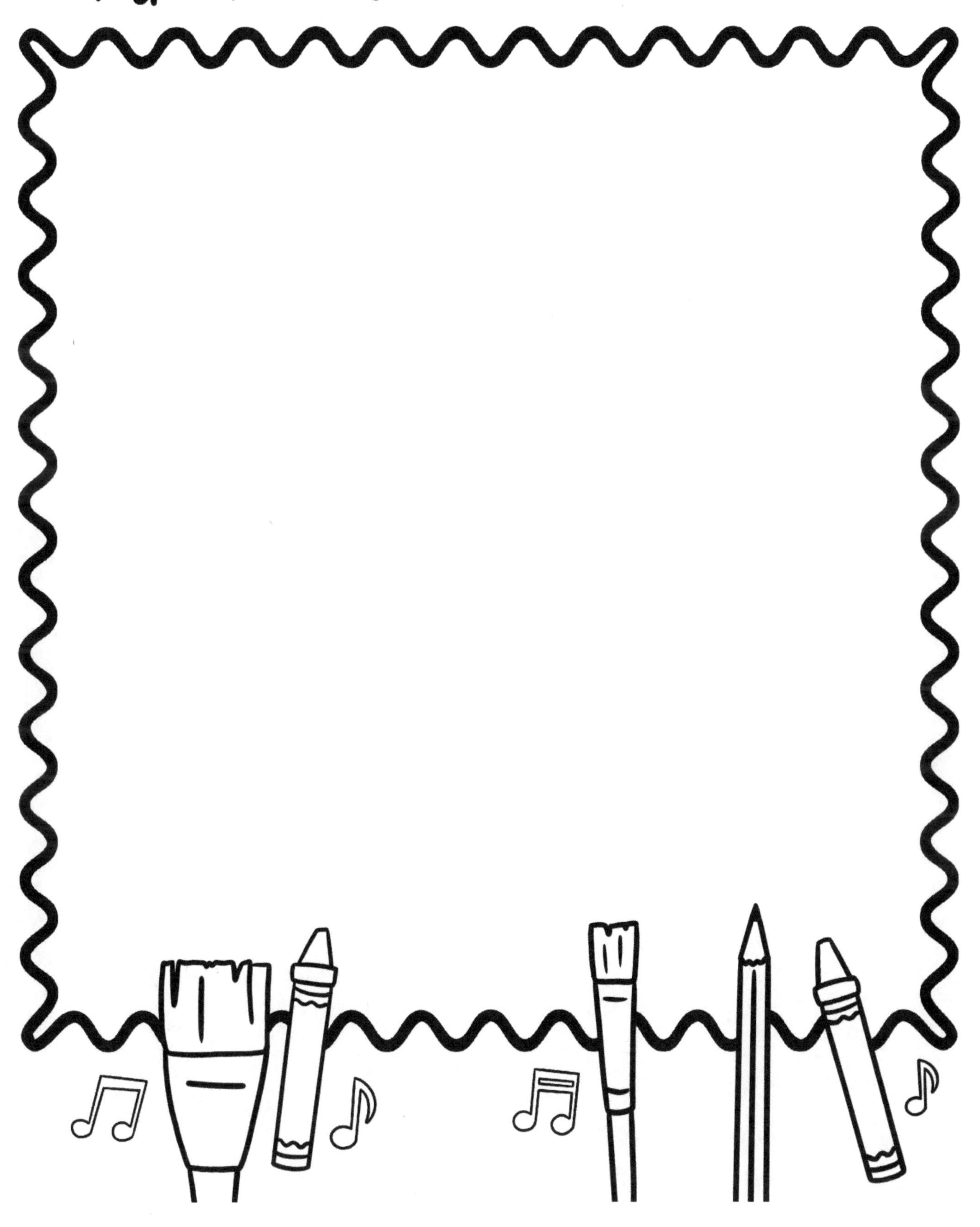

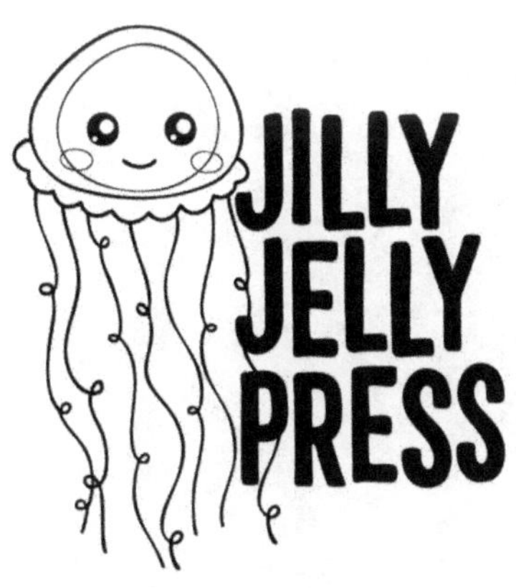
JILLY
JELLY
PRESS

www.ingramcontent.com/pod-product-compliance
Lightning Source LLC
LaVergne TN
LVHW081422110826
845149LV00010B/1836
9798998844300